Buy a Classic Rolls-Royce or Bentley
By Lan Sluder

Copyright

Copyright © 2015 by Lan Sluder
All rights reserved.
ISBN: 978-0-692-43519-9

Published in the United States by Equator.

Although every attempt to provide accurate and timely information was made, no warranty or guarantee for information in this is book is expressed or implied. Opinions expressed are those of the author. Errors, if any, will be corrected in the next edition. In the end the responsibility for buying, selling and owning a Rolls-Royce or Bentley motorcar is up to each individual.

Trademarks used in this book are owned by the respective manufacturers and other businesses and are used for identification purposes only. Photographs and illustrations, if not by the author, are in the public domain, are used under fair use provisions or are used with permission of the copyright owner. Photographs by Sheila M. Lambert are © copyright by Sheila M. Lambert.

The cover spread is of a 1991 Silver Spur II (photo by Lan Sluder).

First Edition

Table of Contents

PREFACE 5

HISTORY OF ROLLS-ROYCE AND BENTLEY 8
    FOUNDING OF ROLLS-ROYCE 8
    THE SILVER GHOST 8
    ROLLING CHASSIS AND COACHBUILDERS 10
    BENTLEY EARLY HISTORY 11
    BETWEEN THE WARS 12
    TAKEOVER OF BENTLEY 15
    THE CREWE YEARS: EARLY POST-WWII VEHICLES 15
    1955-1966: ROLLS-ROYCE SILVER CLOUD AND BENTLEY S-TYPE 19
    1965-1980: ROLLS-ROYCE SILVER SHADOW AND BENTLEY T-SERIES 23
    RECEIVERSHIP 27
    1980-1997: SILVER SPIRIT, SILVER SPUR AND DERIVATIVES 28
    SECOND GENERATION OF SILVER SPIRIT AND SILVER SPUR ... 30
    BENTLEY RESURGENCE 31
    1998-2002: VOLKSWAGEN TAKES OVER 32
    BMW TAKES OVER ROLLS-ROYCE 35
    2003-PRESENT ROLLS-ROYCES AND BENTLEYS 36

ROLLS-ROYCE AND BENTLEY TIME LINE 38

BADGES, MASCOTS AND SYMBOLS 43

WHO OWNS ROLLS-ROYCE AND BENTLEY CARS? 46

FACTORS TO CONSIDER BEFORE BUYING 51

PRICING RULES OF THUMB 55

TWELVE STEPS TO BUYING A ROLLS-ROYCE OR BENTLEY 58

HOW MUCH WILL YOU PAY? 62

SUGGESTED MODELS FOR FIRST-TIME BUYERS 69
    1965-1980 ROLLS-ROYCE SILVER SHADOW AND DERIVATIVES 69
    1980-1989 ROLLS-ROYCE SILVER SPIRIT AND DERIVATIVES 73
    1989-1998 ROLLS-ROYCE SILVER SPIRIT II/SILVER SPUR II AND
    DERIVATIVES 75
    1955-1966 ROLLS-ROYCE SILVER CLOUD I, II AND III 79
    OTHER OPTIONS FOR THE SPECIALIST BUYER 82

CHASSIS NUMBERS AND VIN **84**
FINANCING & INSURING YOUR ROLLS-ROYCE OR BENTLEY. 87
  FINANCING.. 87
  INSURANCE 88
WHERE TO FIND YOUR CAR **90**
  AUCTIONS... 90
  DEALERS 91
  INDIVIDUALS.. 92
SELLING YOUR CAR **94**
ROLLS-ROYCE AND BENTLEY ENTHUSIAST CLUBS **95**
ROLLS-ROYCE AND BENTLEY DEALERSHIPS **102**
  ROLLS-ROYCE..102
  BENTLEY 111
SOURCES OF PARTS, RESTORATION, REPAIRS AND OTHER INFORMATION **125**
  PARTS... 125
  RESTORATIONS AND SPECIALIST REPAIR SERVICE 129
  TECHNICAL CONSULTANTS 135
  TRANSPORT... 135
DICTIONARY OF ROLLS-ROYCE AND BENTLEY TERMS **136**
BIBLIOGRAPHY **147**
ABOUT THE AUTHOR **150**
INDEX **152**

Preface

The author's 1991 Rolls-Royce Silver Spur II   Photo by Sheila M. Lambert

This is the book I wish I had when I bought my Rolls-Royce.

Many, many books have been written on Rolls-Royce and Bentley, and there are people who are absolute experts on the history of each model, down to the chassis numbers produced in such and such a year, or the exact month that Silver Shadows went from six- to five-button radios or Silver Spirits stopped using headlight wipers or whatever.

I am not that person, and information like that is not why you should read this book.

Instead, I am merely a relatively recent Rolls-Royce buyer and owner, one who has made mistakes and who has tried, through research and from talking to other owners and by attending enthusiasts' club events, to learn how to avoid these mistakes the next time.

This book is for the individual who, for whatever reason, is considering the idea of buying and owning a veteran, vintage or classic Rolls-Royce or Bentley.

What I try to do in this book is:

• Give you a general overview of the unique and somewhat complicated history of Rolls-Royce and Bentley.

• Provide a brief thumbnail sketch of the different models and styles of Rolls-Royce and Bentley motorcars, along with in many cases photographs of them. Of course, due to the many different body styles provided by coachbuilders, especially in the pre-World War II period and to some degree afterwards, it is impossible to even begin to show the various body and interior styles.

• Give you an idea of what to consider before buying a Rolls-Royce or Bentley.

• Suggest a handful of Rolls-Royce and Bentley models most suited for a first-time buyer and their typical cost.

• List the steps you should take to buy a specific Rolls-Royce or Bentley motorcar.

• Provide a range of prices, in today's market, that you should expect to pay for any given model of Rolls-Royce or Bentley.

• Let you know what the real cost of owning and maintaining one of these automobiles is likely to be and to explore the ways in which buying, owning and selling the vehicle is bound to have frustrations, complications and headaches, in addition to pleasures.

• Recommend sources of technical expertise, repairs, restoration, shipment and further advice for you as a Rolls-Royce or Bentley buyer or owner.

• Provide suggestions on where you can get more information, if you need it and want it.

I don't have to tell you that Rolls-Royce and Bentley motorcars are special. They turn heads. They are, and have been since the original Rolls-Royce Limited company was established more than a century ago, the choice of royalty and heads of state, and of wealthy business owners and celebrities.

Some new models today cost well over half a million dollars. Yet, you can own and enjoy an extraordinary example of automotive history for as little as the cost of a used Ford or Chevrolet or of a new compact.

But the questions are, "Should I?" and "How?"

Those are the questions I have tried to answer in this book.

Doubtless, mistakes and misstatements have crept into this book, despite my best efforts to provide reliable and accurate information. I would appreciate you correcting me, or in the case of opinions I've offered, for you to provide your own view where it differs from mine. Please email me at lansluder@gmail.com.

Finally, information provided in this little volume should be used with care and common sense, and only after comparing it with the facts and opinions of other authors and owners. In the end, the responsibility for buying, owning and caring for a Rolls-Royce or Bentley is up to the individuals involved.

1952 Bentley Mark VI, entered for judging at the Rolls-Royce Owners' Club national meet in Orlando in 2015   Photo by Sheila M. Lambert

Rolls-Royce and Bentley History

Scores of books have been written on the history of Rolls-Royce and Bentley. Please refer to the Bibliography at the end of this book for references to some of the best of these histories. In this book, I only highlight the key events and developments in the history of these companies and their motorcars.

Founding of Rolls-Royce

The history of what would become the most iconic automobile brand in the world goes back to the early days of English motoring, to May 1904. Two men met for lunch at the Midland Hotel in Manchester. One, Charles Stewart Rolls, had been born into a life of privilege. He studied mechanical engineering at Cambridge, where, according to Rolls-Royce company histories, he was the first undergraduate to own a car. He began racing cars and owned a dealership in Fulham, England, that sold imported cars, mostly from France.

The other, Frederick Henry Royce, the son of a failed flourmill owner, was a self-made man, with only one year of formal education. Royce worked at various jobs until in 1884 when he and a partner opened a company in Manchester that made electrical parts. The company grew and began manufacturing electric motors, cranes and dynamos, but Royce had an interest in automobiles. In 1903, Royce designed and built his first car engine, and in 1904 he produced his first motorcar, a two-cylinder model called the Royce 10. The third buyer of a Royce 10 horsepower car, Henry Edmunds of Glover, had arranged for Royce and Rolls to get together at Manchester.

Just before Christmas in 1904, Rolls and Royce entered in an agreement for Royce to build cars at his Manchester works, which would be sold exclusively at Rolls' dealership in Fulham, under the Rolls-Royce brand name. The first cars were 10 to 30 horsepower models with from two to six cylinders. Even in those early days the little Rolls-Royce cars had a version of the distinctive radiator grill that would be used, in various forms, to the present day.

The Silver Ghost

Soon it was clear a larger factory would be needed to produce cars. Rolls-Royce Limited was established on March 15, 1906. Production began in 1907 at a new factory, designed mostly by Henry Royce, near Derby. An entirely new model, with a 40/50 horsepower, six-cylinder engine, officially termed the **40/50** by Rolls-Royce but popularly known as the **Silver Ghost,** was introduced at the London Motor Show in late 1906. It was only in 1925 that the company officially recognized the Silver Ghost name. This model, in various forms, remained in production until 1926. For nearly all of this period, it was the only model Rolls-Royce sold.

In foreground, green 1907 Rolls-Royce 40/50, or Silver Ghost, is one of the oldest examples of this model still in existence, and it's still running today Photo by Sheila M. Lambert

The car initially had a side-valve six-cylinder, 7,036 cc engine, increased to 7,428 cc in 1910, with the cylinders cast in two units of three cylinders. Each cylinder had two spark plugs. In later models, power output increased from 48 horsepower at 1,250 rpm to 80 horsepower at 2,250 rpm. In the words of the time, the 40/50 had "pistons as big as top hats, going up and down like Otis lifts."

A three-speed transmission was replaced with a four-speed in 1913. Electric lighting became an option in 1914, replacing oil lamps, and became standard in 1919. An automatic electric starter also was introduced in 1919.

The chassis had rigid front and rear axles and leaf springs all around. Early models had brakes on the rear wheels operated by a hand lever, with a pedal-operated transmission brake. The brake system changed to drums on the rear axle in 1913. Four-wheel servo-assisted brakes became optional in 1923.

The Silver Ghost could do 50 mph or more on the highway, more than enough speeds for the roads of that period, and got around 19 miles per U.S. gallon, remarkable for such a heavy vehicle and in fact better mileage than most modern Rolls-Royce motorcars enjoy.

This was the car that established the reputation of Rolls-Royce. It was so silent that sometimes you could not tell when the car was running. It was so steady that you could balance a coin on its edge on the radiator. At a time when cars frequently broke down on the road, the Silver Ghost was extremely reliable, and owners found they could use the car for years without an engine overhaul or major repairs.

Development and sales of the Silver Ghost were suspended during World War I, but the 40/50 chassis and engine were provided to the British Army by Rolls-Royce Armoured Cars.

A total of 6,173 of the Silver Ghosts were produced at Derby and another 1,701 at a U.S. factory in Springfield, Mass., which operated from 1921 to 1931. Many of these motorcars are still in working condition today, and all are highly sought-after collector's cars.

Charles Rolls died in a flying accident in 1910, and Henry Royce was often ill. Claude Goodman Johnson, managing director of Rolls-Royce Ltd. until his death in 1926, kept the company alive and profitable. He was called the "hyphen" in the Rolls-Royce name. It was Johnson's idea to limit the line to one solid, quiet and highly reliable model. Johnson drove a Silver Ghost non-stop around Britain for thousands of miles, proving how reliable it was. An automobile magazine of the time dubbed it "the best car in the world."

Rolling Chassis and Coachbuilders

In a tradition that goes back to days of early 18th century horse-drawn carriages, in the young days of auto manufacturing and indeed generally until after World War II, Rolls-Royce, like many other upper-end car companies, manufactured only the engine, chassis and other mechanical components from the instrument panel forward. Together, this was called the rolling chassis.

Companies called coachbuilders made the bodies and interiors. At one time there were around 60 coachbuilders in the U.K. alone. Among the leading coachbuilders in the early 20th century were Hooper & Co, James Young, Park Ward and H. J. Mulliner. Although Rolls-Royce and its subsidiaries began making pressed-steel bodies in 1946, appearing first on the 1946 **Bentley Mark VI** and 1949 Rolls-Royce **Silver Dawn**, a few custom coachbuilders, both independent and owned by Rolls-Royce, continued to create bespoke Rolls-Royce bodies even as late as the 1980s and 1990s.

Early Silver Ghost rolling chassis with engine alone cost about 1,000 British pounds, equivalent to around 100,000 pounds or US$150,000 today. Coachbuilt bodies and interiors could in some cases cost the buyer that much again in custom work and sometimes took as long as a year to create and fit to the chassis. (Exchange and inflation rates varied over time.)

1929 Bentley "Blower" racing car   From Ralph Lauren collection

Bentley Early History

Bentley Motors Limited was founded in 1919 by Walter Owen (W. O.) Bentley at Cricklewood near London, with its first cars delivered in 1921. From the earliest days, Bentley was known for its heavy but sporty, fast and reliable cars. A group of wealthy British motoring enthusiasts called the "Bentley Boys" was among those who won five Le Mans 24-hour races in Bentleys from 1924 to 1930, along with a number of other prominent speed and endurance races.

Between the Wars

By the early 1920s, improvements to the cars of Rolls-Royce's competitors had resulted in sales of the 40/50 or Silver Ghost declining to nearly one-half the level of earlier years. In response, Rolls-Royce Ltd. in 1926 introduced the **New Phantom.**

1927 Rolls-Royce New Phantom, later call Phantom I

The New Phantom (later called Phantom I when the **Phantom II** was introduced in 1929) had a 7.7-liter overhead valve straight-six. It used the same chassis as the Silver Ghost and like later Ghost models had front and rear springs and servo-assisted brakes. It was manufactured both at Derby and in the U.S. at the Springfield factory. There were a few differences between the English and American models including the use of different transmissions.

As before, only the "rolling chassis" of the Phantom – chassis, engines and mechanical parts from the instrument panel forward – were manufactured by Rolls-Royce Ltd. Coachbuilders that produced bodies for Phantom I cars included Park Ward, H. J. Mulliner, Thrupp & Baberly, Barker and Hooper. American Phantoms could be bought with standardized bodies from Brewster & Co., which was owned by Rolls-Royce. Altogether, 3,509 Phantom I cars were produced, including 1,240 made in the U.S. at Springfield.

A few years earlier, in 1922, Rolls-Royce had introduced the **Twenty**, a smaller and less expensive model meant to appeal to owners who drove their own vehicles, rather than using a chauffeur. The Twenty used a 3,127 cc (3.1-liter) inline six-cylinder motor that could reach a top speed of about 60 mph. The rolling chassis initially sold for around 1,100 pounds, and with coachwork around 1,600 pounds. In today's dollars that represents well over $200,000. A total of 2,940 were delivered.

Later, in 1929, Rolls-Royce brought out the successor to the Twenty, the **20/25**. The 20/25 chassis continued in production until 1936, using a six-cylinder, 3,699 cc engine and a four-speed transmission. Third and fourth gears were synchromesh from 1932 onward. Rolls-Royce manufactured 3,827 of the 20/25s.

That same year, 1929, Rolls-Royce also introduced the **Phantom II**. This Phantom used a version of the original Phantom's 7.7-liter (468 cubic-inch) engine but had an entirely new chassis with a 150-inch wheelbase. A shorter 144-inch wheelbase version also was offered. The front axle was mounted on semi-elliptical leaf springs as on the 40/50, but the rear axle was now also mounted on semi-elliptical leaf springs instead of cantilever springs. This, along with drivetrain changes, allowed the frame to be lower than before, improving the handling. Between 1929 and 1936, 1,767 of the Phantom II rolling chassis were produced at Derby.

In 1936, an updated version of the 20/25 was introduced. It was called the **25/30** and sported a larger 4,257 cc engine. A total of 1,201 of these were manufactured from 1936 to 1938.

That same year, 1936, the **Phantom III** debuted. It marked a major change in the large Rolls-Royces, in that it had an aluminum-alloy overhead valve V-12 engine with a displacement of 7.32 liters or 448 cubic inches. It also was unusual in that it had a twin ignition system, with two distributors, two coils and 24 spark plugs.

A beautiful silver and black 1935 Rolls-Royce 20/25 with coachbuilt body by Hooper
Photo by Sheila M. Lambert

The chassis has independent coil springs in the front and semi-elliptical leaf springs in back. The four-speed transmission was synchromesh in the top three gears. The Phantom III even had its own chassis lubrication system, operated by a lever in the driver's compartment.

This was a large vehicle. With a four-door body by Barker coachbuilders it weighed about 7,700 pounds and got only 8 miles per gallon. The turning radius was 48 feet. It attained a top speed of less than 90 mph and required nearly 17 seconds to get from 0 to 60 mph. In the 1964 James Bond film *Goldfinger* the villain, Auric Goldfinger, drives a Phantom III because he knew it would carry the large weight of gold bars he was smuggling. A total of 715 to 727 Phantom IIIs were produced (numbers reported vary), the last one in 1941 although this final Phantom III was not delivered to its owner until after the war.

The **Wraith**, a Scottish word for ghost, debuted in 1938 and was manufactured in that year and 1939, when British civilian automobile production was disrupted by the war. This vehicle used the same engine as the 25/30 but had a cross-flow cylinder head. The four-speed transmission had synchro added to second gear, in addition to third and fourth. Rolls-Royce produced 492 Wraiths at the Derby factory.

Takeover of Bentley

As a result of the impact of the Great Depression, in 1931 Bentley Motors Ltd. failed and was absorbed into Rolls-Royce Ltd. Production of Bentleys ceased until 1933, when production resumed at the Rolls-Royce factory at Derby. A total of 2,411 Bentleys were manufactured at Derby during this period in the 1930s, including the Bentley 3½-liter, 4¼-liter and Mark V.

The Crewe Years: Early Post-WWII Vehicles

In 1938, Rolls-Royce opened a factory at Crewe, in northwest England, primarily to manufacture airplane engines for the war effort. After World War II, production of both Rolls-Royce and Bentley automobiles was moved to the Crewe facility, which manufactured the two brands until 2002 and, although from 1998 under the ownership of Volkswagen AG, Bentley cars are produced at Crewe to this day.

In the Depression years of the 1930s, sales of Rolls-Royce and Bentley motorcars had slowed, and Rolls-Royce Limited never made a profit during that period. After the war, the company faced new problems, including punitive income tax rates in Britain and a purchase tax that doubled to more than 66% in 1947.

To earn a profit without sacrificing the quality of these luxury cars, Rolls-Royce management decided to "rationalise" (to use the British spelling) the production of the vehicles, by using more standard components that would be interchangeable among different models and a standard chassis frame that was variable in length. The Bentley Mark V that had been introduced in 1939 was to be the first example of this rationalised philosophy, but of course Hitler's aggression interrupted things.

The post-war Silver Dawn was the first Rolls-Royce with all-steel body built by the company as a complete car – this black beauty is a 1954   Photo by Sheila M. Lambert

The second change introduced after the war by Rolls-Royce was the development of a standard steel saloon body of Rolls-Royce's own design, rather than relying so much on outside coachbuilders. All-steel bodies, first used on the **Bentley Mark VI** in 1946 and on Rolls-Royce cars in 1949 on the **Silver Dawn,** were produced by the Pressed Steel Company (later Pressed

Steel Fisher) to Rolls-Royce specifications. The bodies were then fitted to the chassis and with finishings done at the Crewe factory. These were the first complete cars manufactured and assembled by Rolls-Royce at the factory. However, coachbuilders Park Ward (itself by then a subsidiary of Rolls-Royce Limited), H. J. Mulliner, Hooper, James Young and others continued to supply bodies and interiors for many Rolls-Royces after the war. Custom coachwork by top builders typically cost up to 30% more than that of all-steel Pressed Steel bodies.

The all-steel bodies and interiors from Rolls-Royce generally were as luxurious and as well made as those provided by coachbuilders, and the company was able to provide a finished total product at lower cost. The only problem was that the quality of sheet steel available in the early post-war period was not high, and many of the Rolls-Royce and Bentley vehicles produced from 1946 to 1955 eventually suffered serious rust problems. This problem was solved in 1955, when the second generation of standard bodies was introduced, with better steel and aluminum bonnets (hoods), boot (trunk) lids and doors.

Initially during this period the chassis were riveted, but in 1953 welded chassis were introduced. This eliminated the problem of rivets coming loose when the vehicles were driven over rough terrain.

Most of the new standardized cars of the early postwar period used the 4,257 cc six-cylinder engine, whose basic designed dated back to the 20/25 horsepower engine of the early 1920s. The goal, not always achieved, was to have an engine that had a life of at least 100,000 miles before requiring an overhaul.

The **Silver Wraith,** introduced in 1946, was the first major postwar Rolls-Royce. Despite the name, the new Silver Wraith had little in common with the Wraith that has been developed before the war. The 1946 Silver Wraith had a 127-inch wheelbase, compared with a 136-inch wheelbase on the 1939 Wraith, exposed coil springs front suspension and semi-floating rear axle. Front brakes were hydraulic, a first for Rolls-Royce, while the rear brakes were mechanical drums. It had automatic ride control, with the suspension stiffening at higher speeds, with a manual override on the rear dampers only. The six-cylinder overhead inlet valve, side exhaust valve $4\frac{1}{4}$-liter engine had a cast iron block with aluminum cylinder head. The water pump and dynamo were driven by a fan belt, instead of gears.

As noted, the first postwar Bentley, the **Mark VI,** was delivered in the fall of 1946. Though similar to the Silver Wraith, it differed in having a shorter wheelbase of 120 inches and a higher performance engine with two carburetors. A total of 5,202 Mark VIs were sold, making it one of the most popular Bentleys ever.

Silver Wraith production continued until 1958, with modifications to the original design including a larger bore engine, a longer 133-inch wheelbase, welded instead of riveted frame and other changes. With stylish designs by leading coachbuilders, most automobile experts consider the Silver Wraith a considerable improvement over prewar vehicles. A total of 1,883 Silver Wraiths were produced.

Due to conditions in the home market, in the postwar period the export market, especially the United States, became much more important. To that end, the Rolls-Royce **Silver Dawn** was developed and introduced in April 1949. Initially, the Silver Dawn was for export only. It had the then-standard 4,257 cc six-cylinder engine with one carburetor, a radiator grill of new design with 22 fixed shutters, export-type bumpers and left-hand drive. Automatic transmissions produced by General Motors were first offered on the Silver Dawn, initially available for export only and then on domestic models. As tested by *Motor* magazine in 1954, the Silver Dawn with automatic transmission had a top speed of 94 mph and got 12.8 miles to the U.S. gallon.

The Silver Dawn with steel body sold in the U.S. for around $14,000, approximately $135,000 in today's dollars. By comparison, the price of the popular, newly designed American-made 1949 Ford with V-8 engine started at around $1,500, or $14,500 in today's dollars. A total of only 761 Silver Dawns were sold.

The **Bentley Mark VI R-Type** was similar to the Silver Dawn. A total of 2,530 R-Types were produced, including 208 **R-Type Continentals.**

The **Phantom IV** was a very limited production motorcar. Only 18 of these large, deluxe limousines were produced from 1950 to 1956, all with coachbuilt bodies, mostly by H. J. Mulliner and Hooper. Except for one car retained by Rolls-Royce, all were sold exclusively to royalty and heads of state, including Britain's Queen Elizabeth II, Princess Margaret and the Duke of Gloucester, General Franco of Spain (who took delivery of three), the Shah of Persia, King Feisal II of Saudi Arabia and the Sultan of Kuwait, who took two.

Only 18 Rolls-Royce Phantom IV cars were produced and 17 were sold to royalty and heads of state – this one belonged to Aga Khan III of India

1955-1966: Rolls-Royce Silver Cloud and Bentley S-Type

By the mid-1950s, the early postwar Rolls-Royce and Bentley motorcars were beginning to look dated. The solution was the 1955 **Rolls-Royce Silver Cloud** and its Bentley counterpart, the **S-Type**. Except for the grills and name badges, these were the same car.

The chassis of these vehicles, with a 123-inch wheelbase, included a number of small but important improvements, such as 50% more torsional rigidity. Girling "Autostatic" brake systems were used, and for safety from 1956 the system had dual master cylinders and reservoirs. Also in 1956 power steering was first offered as on Rolls-Royce, initially for export only and then domestically. For the first time, automatic transmissions became standard on all models. The Silver Cloud had a General Motors four-speed "Hydromatic" transmission.

Initially, the engine on both the Silver Cloud and Bentley S-Type was a 4.9-liter six-cylinder. In 1959 a 6.2-liter V-8 was introduced. As tested by an automobile magazine of the time, a 1960 Silver Cloud with V-8 had a top speed of 105 mph, acceleration from 0 to 60 in 10.9 seconds and fuel economy of 11 miles per U.S. gallon. Early V-8 engines had a problem with broken crankshafts; the problem was resolved in 1963 with a nitride-hardened crankshaft. Also in 1963 engine compression was increased, and most of the later V-8s required premium-grade, high-octane gasoline.

The elegant, iconic sweep of the Silver Cloud series, first introduced in 1955, says "Rolls-Royce" to many collectors   Photo by Sheila M. Lambert

Perhaps more important than the mechanical improvements were the changes in body styling. The new standard saloon cars, with steel bodies built by the Pressed Steel Company and fitted by Rolls-Royce at its Crewe factory, were sleek and modern-looking. The Silver Cloud and S-Type had higher-quality 20-gauge zinc-plated steel to resist rust; an aluminum alloy was used for bonnet, boot lid and doors.

The Cloud and S-Type cars were larger than the Silver Wraith, with spacious and comfortable bench seats front and rear. The seats were covered in Connolly leather, and carpets were deep-pile Wilson. There were folding picnic tables with fine wood veneer on the backs of the front seats, lighted vanity mirrors, cigarette lighters and ashtrays front and rear and a push-button radio. Later editions had air-conditioning and electric windows. A long-wheelbase version with 127-inch wheelbase became available in 1957.

BUY A CLASSIC ROLLS-ROYCE OR BENTLEY

David Oglivy, the British-born genius behind Oglivy & Mather ad agency, created this famous 1959 print ad for the Silver Cloud

Even by today's standards, the Silver Cloud and Bentley S-Type were luxurious, impressive and comfortable vehicles. At the time, they really had no serious competition in their category. The early Clouds of the 1950s sold for around $14,000 in the United States, about $113,000 in today's dollars. By comparison, the Chevrolet Corvette went for under $4,000 at the time.

David Ogilvy, the British-born, Oxford-educated advertising copywriter and marketing genius at Ogilvy & Mather advertising agency in New York, created print advertisements for Rolls-Royce that helped give it a unique brand image beyond Britain. The headline of one famous ad read, "At 60 miles an hour the loudest noise in the new Rolls-Royce comes from the electric clock."

In 1959, with the introduction of the more powerful 6.2-liter (378 cubic-inch) V-8 engine, Rolls-Royce was able to offer a large, stately limousine, the **Phantom V.** This seven-passenger, chauffeur-driven car was sold in several different coachbuilt designs by Mulliner, Park Ward and James Young. A total of 516 Phantom Vs were produced from 1959 to 1968. Phantom V owners included Queen Elizabeth II and the Queen Mother, the Shah of Iran, John Lennon of the Beatles, King Olav V of Norway, Yugoslav President Josip Tito and the Governor of Hong Kong.

Stunning 1962 Bentley S2 drophead coupé Photo by Sheila M. Lambert

Among the most-popular vehicles made by Rolls-Royce Limited up to that time, a total of 7,372 Silver Clouds were produced from 1955 to 1966. The Silver Cloud I with six-cylinder engine was in production from 1955 to 1958, the Silver Cloud II with V-8 from 1959 to 1962 and the Silver Cloud III with V-8 from 1963 to 1966. The comparable Bentley S-Types were the S1, 2 and 3. All together, 6,310 of these Bentleys were produced. During this period, sales of Bentleys began to fall behind sales of Rolls-Royce. Most viewed the Bentley of this period as simply a Rolls-Royce with a different radiator grill and a different name badge.

1965-1980: Rolls-Royce Silver Shadow and Bentley T-Series

In the fall of 1965, Rolls-Royce Limited announced what it claimed were the most radically different motorcars in the then 59-year history of the company, the **Rolls-Royce Silver Shadow** and the **Bentley T-Series**.

In many ways, this was a valid claim. The new cars certainly were different from any previous model. They had a chassisless monocoque (pronounced mono-coke) or unibody construction, innovative technical advances including self-leveling independent suspension and a complex hydraulic brake system with disc brakes and refinements such as power seats. The styling was modern, yet classic enough that it endured for a decade and a half, very different from the Detroit approach of making major styling changes every year or two.

With its Bentley T-Series cousin, the Silver Shadow had a version of the Rolls-Royce V-8 engine introduced in 1959, initially a 6,230 cc or 6.2-liter displacement, but from July 1970 the V-8's stroke was increased to deliver 6,750 ccs or 412 cubic inches.

The Shadow and its immediate derivatives remained in production for 15 years, with a total of more than 37,000 of them delivered, outselling any previous model. Some vehicles, such as the Corniche (based originally on the Silver Shadow), were so in demand that at times buyers had to pay a premium of up to 80% over the list price.

The Silver Shadow was particularly popular in the United States, where it was considered a "compact," at least compared with other luxury cars. The initial Silver Shadow and T-Series models had a 119½-inch wheelbase and an overall length bumper to bumper of about 17 feet. By comparison, the 1965 Cadillac Fleetwood Brougham had an overall length of almost 19 feet on a 133-

inch wheelbase, and the solidly middle-class 1965 Chevrolet Impala had an overall length of 17 feet, 9 inches on a 119-inch wheelbase.

Introduced in 1965, the Silver Shadow was the first "modern" Rolls-Royce, with monocoque construction, disc brakes and improved handling -- it proved the most popular Rolls-Royce in the company's history   Photo by Sheila M. Lambert

The long-wheelbase Silver Shadow model, introduced in 1969, had a 123½-inch wheelbase and an overall length of 17 feet 3½ inches.

However, despite the shorter wheelbase and overall length, the Silver Shadow and Bentley T-Series actually had more interior room and larger boots (trunks) than earlier Rolls-Royce and Bentley vehicles.

The unibody construction had separate front and rear subframes. Most vehicles used a body base unit provided to Rolls-Royce by Pressed Steel Fisher. The doors, fenders and other body panels were welded to the base unit, which made for a strong and fairly rigid body. H. J. Mulliner and Park Ward, coachbuilders now owned by Rolls-Royce, used a slightly different version of the body base unit for their coachbuilt models.

The front suspension was independent coil springs, and the rear had independent coil springs with trailing arms and hydraulic dampers. The hydraulic system used two camshaft-driven pumps delivering brake fluid at up to 2,500 psi to a pair of accumulators on the side of the crankcase. The hydraulic pressure was used both for braking and for automatic leveling and height control system, keeping the car the same height regardless of load. The Silver Shadow/T-Series had four-wheel 11-inch disc brakes. Wheels were 15-inch steel, carrying 8.45 x 15 low-profile tires. Later models used radial ply tires.

Fascia and interior of a 1972 right-hand drive Silver Shadow

The steering was power-assisted, and later models used a rack-and-pinion steering. The automatic transmission in British models was a four-speed, but the automatic transmission in U.S. and other export cars was the reliable and proven General Motors three-speed, used by Rolls-Royce until late 1990. Interiors remained as luxurious as ever, with flawless Connolly leather, burr walnut veneers and deep-pile lamb's wool carpets.

Over the course of the 15 years they were produced, many incremental changes and improvements were made, but the essential styling and engineering remained basically unchanged.

During the early and mid-1970s, two new derivative models of the Shadow debuted, the **Corniche** in March 1971 and the **Camargue** in March 1975. The Corniche, from the French for a coastal road, was produced in a two-door coupe (or coupé) version and as a two-door convertible. The convertible or drophead version proved very popular – then and still today, as collector's cars – and more than 3,200 of the soft tops were produced from 1971 to 1987, and by 1995 more than 5,000 of the convertible Corniche models had been delivered, plus more than 1,000 two-door hard top coupés. The Corniche was sold in some markets until 1986 and in others until 1988.

1986 Rolls-Royce Corniche II drophead coupé   Photo by Sheila M. Lambert

The Corniche II was produced from 1986, the Corniche III from 1989 and the Corniche IV from 1992. A different car, the Corniche V, was developed and sold in 2000-2001 under the Volkswagen AG regime. From 1971 to 1984, a small number (about 140) of **Bentley Corniche** cars were sold; in 1984 the name was changed to **Bentley Continental,** with production of 421 Continentals through 1994, plus another 8 Bentley Continental Turbo cars from 1992 to 1995.

The Camargue, named after part of the Rhone region in France, had body styling by Italian coachbuilder Pininfarina, an aircraft-style fascia and the world's first automatic split-level air-conditioning system. In today's dollars it cost more than $600,000, arguably the most expensive production Rolls-Royce of all time. Perhaps in part because of its cost, it did not sell very well, with only 531 produced over 11 models years (1975-1986). In 2010, readers of Canada's

Globe & Mail newspaper rated the Camargue as one of the "10 worst cars" in history.

In 1977 the company believed that the number of changes in all of its cars merited a name change, so in that year the Silver Shadow II, Bentley T2 and Silver Wraith II, the long-wheelbase version of the Shadow, were introduced.

Although the vast majority of Rolls-Royces and Bentleys built during this period were the new chassisless design, one old-style holdover remained – the Phantom limousine. The Rolls-Royce **Phantom VI** was officially introduced in early 1969. In design – most bodies were coachbuilt by Mulliner Park Ward on the Rolls-Royce chassis – the Phantom VI retained the 1940s look. Only 374 of these vehicles were built and delivered from 1969 to 1992, mostly to heads of state. One version was armored, adding an extra 1,575 pounds of 7 mm steel plus 50 mm-thick glass.

Receivership

At the height of Rolls-Royce's success with the Silver Shadow, part of the company ran into deep financial difficulty. This had nothing to do with the motorcar division. The company's aero engine division blew up, as its aircraft engine division stumbled in trying to produce a jet engine for the Lockheed L-1011 TriStar.

Rolls-Royce had been manufacturing airplane engines since 1914, and about one-half of the aircraft engines used by the Allies in World War I were made by Rolls-Royce. The legendary Rolls-Royce Merlin engine, partially designed by Henry Royce himself in the early 1930s, powered many of World War II's iconic airplanes, including the Supermarine Spitfire, which was instrumental in winning the Battle of Britain, and the American P-51 Mustang, which used a Merlin engine manufactured by Packard under license from Rolls-Royce.

After World War II, the aero division of Rolls-Royce's became a world leader in turbine and jet engines.

However, when it became the primary developer and provider of a new jet engine for the Lockheed TriStar jumbo jet, Rolls-Royce bit off more than it could chew. Technical difficulties grew more and more serious, and in 1971 Rolls-Royce Limited, which had produced both Rolls-Royce and Bentley motorcars and aircraft engines, was forced into receivership. To save the company, the British government nationalized it.

The motorcar division eventually, in 1980, was sold as Rolls-Royce Motors Ltd. to Vickers and separated from the aero division, which continued as Rolls-Royce Limited. Later, in 1987, under the Margaret Thatcher government, Rolls-Royce Limited was re-privatized as Rolls-Royce PLC.

Rolls-Royce Motors Ltd. continued to produce Rolls-Royce and Bentley automobiles. It remained solvent and profitable. Indeed, just after it was separated from the aero division, it introduced in March 1971 one of its most famous modern models, the Corniche.

1980-1997: Silver Spirit, Silver Spur and Derivatives

Following the successful 15-year run of the Silver Shadow series, Rolls-Royce Motors Ltd. in October 1980 introduced a new line, the **Silver Spirit.**

The Silver Spirit was evolutionary, not revolutionary. It was based on the Silver Shadow II. It used the Silver Shadow II's engine and drive train but with a different rear suspension and a hydraulic system that used mineral oil rather than regular hydraulic fluid. The Silver Shadow II was replaced by the **Silver Spirit,** the Silver Wraith II by the **Silver Spur** (the long-wheelbase version of the Spirit) and the Bentley T2 by the **Mulsanne.**

The Silver Spirit series had a more contemporary, modern styling. It had one-third larger glass area. It was three inches longer and two inches wider than the Silver Shadow series and in fact looked even larger.

In mechanical and technical terms, the Silver Spirit and its derivatives had improved handling and road holding, due to an improved suspension. Drivers noticed that the new Silver Spirit was quieter than the Silver Shadow series. Fuel injection was introduced from 1980 for U.S. and Japanese models, and for cars sold in all parts of the world by 1987.

The replacement of regular hydraulic fluid by mineral oil had several claimed benefits: It was less corrosive if spilled by accident on the car body, had better lubricating qualities and did not absorb water, so it is less corrosive to the seals and lines. On the other hand, it had one big negative: The accidental introduction of even a tiny amount of regular hydraulic fluid into a mineral oil system, or of mineral oil into a regular hydraulic system, will damage the system, resulting in a cost of tens of thousands of dollars to completely rebuild.

Warning signs in several languages are posted prominently in the engine compartment of vehicles that use mineral oil.

A 1982 Rolls-Royce Camargue, shown here at a Bonhams & Butterfields Auction in 2005 – the Camargue was named one of the 10 worst cars in history in a poll of Globe & Mail *readers in Canada*   Photo by Jagvar

While the general appearance and technical details of the Silver Spirit models stayed much the same during the 1980s, continuous small improvements were introduced during the decade, with 1987 seeing the most changes. As noted, from 1987 Silver Spirits sold anywhere in the world were fitted with fuel injection, and electrical changes for 1987 included a new alternator and a smaller but more powerful Japanese-produced starter motor. Anti-locking (ABS) brakes all were introduced for most markets in 1987, and a memory system for power front seats was fitted.

Second Generation of Silver Spirit and Silver Spur

In late 1989 for the 1990 model year, the **Silver Spirit II** and the long-wheelbase **Silver Spur II** were introduced. The biggest change in the II series models was an improved automatic ride control and self-leveling system, controlled by a microprocessor. Alloy wheels also were introduced. Safety was improved with a driver-side airbag. In addition, some comfort and appearance amenities debuted, such as an excellent 10-speaker sound system, automatic parking brake release, electrically adjustable rear seats (in the long-wheelbase Silver Spur II), mobile telephones in front and rear armrests, a remotely operated anti-theft system and a new style of wood veneers with boxwood crossbanding in addition to the burr walnut.

A limited-production **Silver Spur II Touring Limousine,** two feet longer than the regular Silver Spur II, was launched in the fall of 1991, with 10" color television, tape player, CD, 10 extra speakers and a cocktail cabinet.

Unfortunately, a world recession in the early 1990s, which was especially severe in the United States, contributed to a decline in Rolls-Royce and Bentley sales. Around that time, Rolls-Royce Motors Ltd. needed to sell at least 3,000 vehicles a year to sustain profitability. It had achieved sales of around that number every year from 1986 through 1990, including part of the 1991 model year, when total sales for calendar year 1990 reached 3,274. But in 1991, sales dropped by one-half to 1,610 and stayed at around that number or fewer through 1998. Sales in 1992 were at a modern low of 1,244 but did rebound to 1,918 in 1997 before dropping back to a little over 1,600 in 1998.

In 1993, a significantly revised line of Spirit series cars was introduced, including the **Silver Spirit III** and **Silver Spur III.** The main change was a new version of the 6.7-liter V-8, one with considerably more power, enabling a top speed of 130 mph for Rolls-Royces and even higher for the turbocharged Bentley. Airbags became standard for both front seat passenger and driver. The air-conditioning was changed to use CFC-free refrigerant. (Many older vehicles had been retrofitted with the CFC-free refrigerant.)

Although Bentley had offered turbocharging for years, the first turbocharged Rolls-Royce was the **Flying Spur** in 1994, which sold quickly although production was low. A confusing myriad of other models and nameplates were originated in the 1990s. In 1995, the Roman numeral designations were dropped, and Rolls-Royce names reverted to just Silver Spirit, Silver Spur and the slightly less expensive Silver Dawn.

The Silver Spirit or SZ series, introduced in 1980 with a second generation in 1989, was the last of the "true" Rolls-Royce motorcars– this is one of the later versions, a Silver Spur III
Photo by Kristofer Scheiderbauer

Bentley Resurgence

To back up a bit, one significant change in the 1980s was the resurgence of the Bentley brand. For years, Bentley had simply been a rebadged Rolls-Royce. At one point, sales of Bentleys fell to just 5% of that of Rolls-Royce, whereas in the early post-World War II years at Crewe Bentley sales comprised nearly two-thirds of the total sales of Rolls-Royce Limited.

With the introduction of the **Bentley Mulsanne** in 1980, Bentley began to enjoy a revival that would eventually lead it to again outselling Rolls-Royce. Quite quickly, Bentley sales rose to about 40% of total production and by the early 1990s reached about one-half of total production.

This revival of Bentley was achieved in several ways. One was simply in marketing, by branding and advertising the Bentley as its own unique product. For example, the Mulsanne name was a nod to the early success of Bentley on the racing circuit, when Bentley cars from 1924 to 1930 won five 24-Hour Le

Mans endurance races. The Mulsanne Straight was the stretch of the Le Mans racecourse where cars reached their highest speeds.

What truly changed the fortunes of Bentley was the turbocharger, introduced first in 1982 on the Mulsanne (which until then was otherwise similar to the Silver Spirit). Then the **Bentley Eight** was introduced in 1984 at a price point (50,000 British pounds) that was lower than any other Rolls-Royce product of the time.

In 1985 Rolls-Royce Motors Cars Ltd. introduced the **Bentley Turbo R** (R stood for Roadhandling), a fast, sporty four-door sedan that was different in handling and performance than any Rolls-Royce. The Garrett "AiRearch" turbocharger pressurized the air supply to the four-barrel carburetors, increasing the power output by as much a 50%. The Turbo R also had a stiffer front suspension and a sportier look. Early models cost $195,000 in the U.S.

Rolls-Royce in 1991 launched the **Bentley Continental R,** the first Bentley since 1963 that did not share its body styling with Rolls-Royce. The Continental R sold in the U.K. for as much as 175,000 pounds including taxes, a staggering amount at the time. The Continental R also was turbocharged. It had a top speed of 145 mph and could accelerate from 0 to 60 in just 6.6 seconds, amazingly strong performance for a heavy luxury car.

1998-2002: Volkswagen Takes Over

Facing lower sales and economic headwinds, and with its main Rolls-Royce cars aging and lagging the luxury competition in engineering and styling, the company reduced costs where possible. A radical restructuring of the manufacturing process at the Crewe factory, including large layoffs, made it possible for the company to be profitable while delivering as few as 1,300 or 1,400 vehicles a year.

Still, rumors persisted of a possible takeover of Rolls-Royce Motors Ltd. by a German or Japanese company.

In July 1998, it actually happened. Rolls-Royce Motors Ltd., was sold by Vickers PLC to Volkswagen AG, the company that had built is reputation on the little "people's car," the VW Beetle. However, the story is more complex than that and doesn't end there.

When the aircraft engine and motorcar divisions of Rolls-Royce Ltd. were split in the early 1970s due to the financial fiasco in developing the

Lockheed jet engine, ownership of the Rolls-Royce name and main trademarks were vested, not in the part that made cars but in the aircraft engine division. The Rolls-Royce name was only licensed to the motorcar division, and there was a provision that the motorcar company, being considered the very essence of "Britishness," could not be foreign-owned or controlled.

Vickers itself did not object to the sale of Rolls-Royce Motors Ltd. to a foreign buyer, and it obtained legal advice that seemed to allow that, but it preferred that the foreign buyer be BMW, not Volkswagen, as Vickers had been partnering with BMW on jet engines. BMW made an initial lowball offer, then raised it to 340 million pounds. VW, however, made a much higher offer of a reported 430 million pounds, plus an additional sum for Cosworth Engineering, which also was owned by Vickers.

After acquiring the business, Volkswagen spent 500 million pounds (about US$845 million then) to modernize the Crewe factory and increase production capacity. Employment at Crewe more than doubled, to around 3,500.

Altogether, VW likely spent the equivalent of nearly $2 billion U.S. dollars (nearly $4 billion in today's dollars) to make the acquisition, including acquisition costs plus expansions and improvements to the Crewe facilities.

To make a long story shorter, the upshot was the so-called "golf course deal," reportedly called such because it was put together on a golf course in Germany. The deal called for the following:

• VW would buy Rolls-Royce Motors Ltd. in 1998 and build Rolls-Royce and Bentley cars using Rolls-Royce employees at the Crewe factory until 2002.

• After 2002, BMW, having created a new Rolls-Royce car subsidiary, would manufacture a new Rolls-Royce of its own design at a new location. BMW would have the Rolls-Royce name and principal trademarks, but it would create its own new car that would be called Rolls-Royce but have no direct connection with the original Rolls-Royce Limited of 1906 or Rolls-Royce Motors Ltd. established after the split with the aero division.

• Rolls-Royce Motors Ltd. would be renamed Bentley Motors Ltd. and after 2002 would continue to build Bentleys, under VW ownership, at Crewe.

A new model of Rolls-Royce, called the **Silver Seraph,** was announced in 1998 by VW management. Although built at Crewe from 1998 to 2002, using many long-time Rolls-Royce employees, the Silver Seraph was powered by a V-12 engine sourced from BMW, and it had a five-speed transmission. It did have the traditional Connolly leather, Wilson carpets and burr walnut veneer luxury interior of traditional Rolls-Royces. Thus, it had the exterior trappings of Rolls-Royce but with a German engine, and it was produced by a company controlled by VW. The car had a base price of 155,175 pounds in the UK and $220,695 in the U.S. A total of 1,570 Silver Seraphs were produced.

The "oddball" Rolls-Royce Silver Seraph, made at Crewe from 1998 to 2002 by Volkswagen and powered by a BMW V-12 engine

A Bentley counterpart of the Silver Seraph in 1998 was the **Bentley Arnage**, with a twin-supercharged 4.4-liter V-8 sourced from BMW. For the 1999 model year it was designated as the Arnage "Green Label." For the 2000 model year, launched in October 1999, things changed. Due to VW's reluctance to be dependent on its competitor BMW for the engine, an Arnage powered by the venerable Rolls-Royce 6.75-liter V-8 engine, but supercharged, replaced the BMW-powered Arnage. This model was designated the Arnage "Red Label." By 2001, all Arnages were powered by the classic Rolls-Royce V-8, although tweaked by VW engineers. Confused yet?

Also produced by VW in 1999 was the **Bentley Continental T Mulliner** and from 1999-2002 the **Bentley Azure Mulliner**.

An extended wheelbase Rolls-Royce Phantom manufactured by BMW, shown as part of a fleet of 14 limousines purchased by the Peninsula Hotel in Hong Kong in 2006

BMW Takes Over Rolls-Royce

After 2002, BMW got the Rolls-Royce name and primary trademarks, for which it paid a reported 40 million pounds in licensing fees. Its first model, the **Phantom,** was delivered in early 2003. It's unclear where the first BMW Phantoms were actually manufactured but later in 2003 BMW opened a new Rolls-Royce plant at Goodwood, West Sussex, for Phantom production. The "new" Rolls-Royce cars were designed and partially built in Germany at BMW's Dingolfing plant. The V-12 engine, transmission, brakes, electronics and even most of the body were manufactured in Germany. Only the final assembly was done in Goodwood.

Bentley Motors Ltd., owned by Volkswagen, continued to manufacture Bentley cars at Crewe. The last Bentley with a Rolls-Royce engineering heritage was produced in late 2008. It was the Bentley Arnage with a turbocharged version of the 6.75-litre V-8 that can trace its lineage back to the 1959 Silver Cloud and Phantom V.

2003-Present Rolls-Royces and Bentleys

Today, both Rolls-Royce and Bentley cars remain in production as super-premium luxury motorcars. As noted, Bentley is a subsidiary of VW AG, with production at Crewe, and Rolls-Royce is a subsidiary of BMW, with most design and production by BMW in Germany and assembly at Goodwood, England.

A variety of new models have been added over the years. Among the models produced by Bentley/VW today are these:

Mulsanne is Bentley's top-of-the-line model, with a base price of around $300,000. The high-performance version for 2015, the **Mulsanne Speed,** has even more of everything. With a twin turbo 6.7-liter V-8 producing 530 horsepower, it has a claimed top speed of 190 mph. It takes only 4.7 seconds to get from zero to 60 mph. The Speed gets 12 mpg in city driving, 19 on the highway and a combined 14 mpg.

Bentley also offers the more economical **Continental GT,** which starts at around $190,000. There's also the **Grand Convertible** and the **Bentley Flying Spur**. A Bentley SUV, the **Bentayga,** has been announced for 2016, with an expected price of under $300,000.

Volkswagen must be doing something right with its Bentley line, as Bentley sales in 2014 reached an all-time high of just over 11,000, and it received 4,000 pre-orders for the new Bentayga SUV.

Among the models currently offered by Rolls-Royce/BMW are vehicles in three "families," Phantom, Ghost and Wraith.

The top-of-the-line BMW/Rolls-Royce **Phantom** series includes four models, the regular four-door, five-seat Phantom with a BMW 6.7-liter V-12 and eight-speed transmission and a top speed of 150 mph, providing 11 mpg city and 19 mpg highway, even though it weighs almost three tons; an extended wheelbase Phantom on a 150-inch wheelbase, with an overall length of about 20 feet, definitely designed to be chauffeur-driven; a two-door Coupé; and a Drophead Coupé convertible.

The flagship Phantoms have a mostly aluminum alloy body and spaceframe produced in Norway, Denmark and Germany, with final assembly at Goodwood in West Sussex. Rolls-Royce wants to make each car bespoke, so buyers can specify virtually any customization, including a choice of 44,000 paint colors.

The Phantom base price starts at around $400,000, with the extended wheelbase edition around $550,000.

The slightly smaller **Ghost II** (the original modern Ghost was first introduced in 2009) also has the BMW 6.7-liter V-12 and eight-speed transmission, and with the lower weight the powertrain moves the car even faster, reaching 60 mph from a standing start in just 4.7 seconds. The **Wraith** is the two-door coupe sibling of the Ghost. These cars, intended in most cases to be owner-driven, start at around $300,000.

In 2015, BMW/Rolls-Royce announced that a new Rolls-Royce superpremium SUV with all-aluminum body would be offered, likely for the 2016 model year.

Note that many Rolls-Royce dealers today only service 2003 and later models, with new parts provided by BMW. Many Bentley dealers, as heir to the original Rolls-Royce Limited and Rolls-Royce Motors Limited lineage, service pre-2003 Rolls-Royces, with new Crewe parts provided through Volkswagen.

Steering wheel and fascia of 2015 Rolls-Royce Serenity Phantom   Photo Courtesy of Rolls-Royce

Rolls-Royce and Bentley Time Line

Sir Henry Royce, co-founder of Rolls-Royce, from a painting in the National Archives of the U.K.

1904 Charles Stewart Rolls and Frederick Henry Royce meet for lunch at Midlands Hotel in Manchester

1906 Rolls-Royce Limited established by Charles Rolls and Henry Royce, with initial production in Manchester; a 10 horsepower car, originally developed by Royce in 1904, was sold under the Rolls-Royce name

1907 Production of the Rolls-Royce 40/50 horsepower model, later called the Silver Ghost, begins at Manchester

1908 First Rolls-Royce rolling chassis built at new Rolls-Royce factory in Derby

1910 Charles Rolls dies in a flying accident

1919 Walter Owen Bentley founds Bentley Motors Limited

1921 Rolls-Royce factory in Springfield, Mass., opens with production continuing until 1931 (the Springfield facility was razed by its owner, a company called Titeflex, in 2011)

1922 First overhead-valve engine produced, fitted to new Twenty rolling chassis

1926 New Phantom (later called Phantom I) introduced

1929 Phantom II and a smaller Rolls-Royce, the 20/25, debut

1931 Rolls-Royce absorbs Bentley Motors Ltd. after Bentley's failure in the Depression

1933 Rolls-Royce produces the first "Rolls-Bentley," the 3 1/2-liter "Silent Sportscar"

1936 Rolls-Royce 25/30 and the V-12 Phantom III introduced

1939 Bentley Mark V introduced, with limited production at the new Rolls-Royce factory at Pyms Lane, Crewe, Staffordshire, until the war interrupted automobile manufacturing

1939-1945 Rolls-Royce provides aircraft engines, notably the Merlin 27-liter V-12, for the British war effort, with production at Crewe; from this point Rolls-Royce changes from an automobile company that also makes aircraft engines to an aircraft engine company that builds motorcars

1946 New "rationalised" motorcar production system introduced, with more standardized parts, a standard chassis and improved six-cylinder engine, along with an all-steel body (available on the Bentley Mark VI in 1946 and on the Rolls-Royce Silver Dawn starting in 1949); the new Silver Wraith debuts with production continuing at Crewe until 1959

1949 First left-hand drive models, the Rolls-Royce Silver Dawn and Bentley Mark VI, introduced for overseas markets with driving on the right side of the road

1950 Phantom IV limousine introduced for royalty and heads of state, with only 18 produced through 1955

1952 Automatic transmission (from General Motors) offered

1955 Rolls-Royce Silver Cloud and Bentley S-Type introduced with most bodies by Pressed Steel of Cowley near Oxford; the sleek, modern Silver Cloud

I, II and III and Bentley S1, 2 and 3 were produced until 1966; in a change from the previous two decades, Rolls-Royce sales now outpace those of Bentley

The Silver Wraith was the first post-WWII Rolls-Royce, produced from 1946 to 1959 – this 1955 model is a touring limousine with body by H. J. Mulliner Photo by Sheila M. Lambert

1956 Power-assisted steering offered, first on export models and then on all vehicles

1959 A new V-8 engine that would provide, with various changes and improvements, the power for Rolls-Royce and Bentley cars for more than 40 years, introduced; the large, stately Rolls-Royce Phantom V limousine introduced

1965 Rolls-Royce Silver Shadow and Bentley T-Series introduced, claimed to be the most fundamentally changed vehicles in the 59-year history of the company; the new models have a sleek, modern style and the first monocoque or unibody construction without a separate chassis; derivative models in the series later include the Corniche, Camargue, Silver Shadow II and Silver Wraith II; around 40,000 Rolls-Royce and Bentley Shadow-based vehicles are sold during the 15-year production run, of which about 94% were Rolls-

Royces, making the Silver Shadow the most popular series in Rolls-Royce history

1971 Though profitable, Rolls-Royce Limited goes into receivership, due to the soaring cost of its aero engine division in developing a new jet engine for Lockheed L-1011 TriStar wide body jets; the receiver separates the motor car operations from the aero engine division; Rolls-Royce and Bentley Corniche models introduced

1973 A new public company, Rolls-Royce Motors Ltd., is formed, and continues to produce Rolls-Royce and Bentley vehicles at the Crewe facility

1975 A "Centenary Rolls-Royce" produced; Camargue model introduced

1978 Sales of Rolls-Royce models hit 3,357, the highest annual sales level until 2011, after the 2003 takeover by BMW

1980 Vickers PLC, a British engineering and armaments company with roots dating to 1828, acquires Rolls-Royce Motors Ltd.; new Rolls-Royce Silver Spirit line introduced, based on the Silver Shadow II but with a different rear suspension and a hydraulic system that uses mineral oil rather than regular hydraulic fluid; the Silver Shadow II is replaced by the Silver Spirit, the Silver Wraith II by the Silver Spur and the Bentley T2 by the Mulsanne; 17-digit/letter Vehicle Identification Number (VIN) system introduced by the U.S. National Highway Traffic Safety Administration and adopted by Rolls-Royce Motors

1982 Bentley introduces a supercharged version of its Mulsanne, and the Bentley brand enjoys resurgence, with Bentley cars growing to 40% of total production at Crewe later in the 1980s

1985 Bentley Turbo R introduced, further boosting Bentley sales

1989 Silver Spirit II and long wheelbase Silver Spur II introduced for the 1990 model year; driver side airbags are standard

1991 Due to a worldwide recession, sales of Rolls-Royce and Bentley cars for the 1992 model year decline by about one-half from peak of 3,274 in 1990; sales continue in the 1,400-1,900 range annually through the 1990s, but layoffs and new production efficiencies at Crewe enable Rolls-Royce Motors Ltd. to operate profitably at the lower sales level

1993 Silver Spirit III and Silver Spur III models introduced, representing continued evolution of the Spirit and Spur line, notably with a more powerful V-8 engine

1994 First turbocharged Rolls-Royce introduced, the Flying Spur

1995 Rolls-Royce drops the Roman numeral designations and reverts to just the Silver Spirit and Silver Spur names, adding a less expensive Silver Dawn model

1997 Rumors continue that Rolls-Royce Motors Ltd. would be sold, perhaps to a Japanese or German company

1998 Volkswagen AG buys Rolls-Royce Motors, Ltd. and its Rolls-Royce and Bentley lines from Vickers, which preferred to sell to its aircraft engine partner BMW, but VW's offer was higher; the "golf course agreement" between VW and BMW was that VW would continue producing Rolls-Royce (the Silver Seraph) and Bentley cars (beginning with the Arnage) at Crewe through 2002 and Bentleys only thereafter; BMW would license the Rolls-Royce name and principal trademarks and in 2003 begin producing Rolls-Royce badged cars based on German engineering with BMW engines but with traditional Rolls-Royce quality coachwork and interiors, with assembly in England

2002 VW AG sells rights to the Rolls-Royce name and trademarks to BMW AG

2003 BMW begins to assemble Rolls-Royce cars, the Phantom being the first car introduced, at a new plant in Goodwood, England, but the basic body, engine and most mechanical parts are engineered, designed and built in Germany

2008 Final Bentley, the Arnage, with a true Rolls-Royce tradition and the Rolls-Royce V-8 whose origin dated back 50 years, produced at Crewe by Volkswagen

2014 Sales of VW's Bentleys worldwide reach an all-time annual record of 11,020, with the United States and China being the largest markets, and sales of BMW's Rolls-Royce hit an all-time annual record of 4,063

2015 VW/Bentley announces its first SUV, the Bentayga, will be offered in the 2016 model year, and BMW/Rolls-Royce announces plans for its own super-luxury SUV

Badges, Mascots and Symbols

Both Rolls-Royce and Bentley have long sported well-known badges on the radiators. The Spirit of Ecstasy of Rolls-Royce, often also called The Flying Lady, is the better known. In the early years of Rolls-Royce, in the fashion of the day it was called a mascot.

Although there is some disagreement about its exact provenance, a well-known artist and sculptor of the time, Charles Robinson Sykes, designed the Spirit of Ecstasy in 1910, with a revised version in 1911.

The model for the fairy-like creation, a woman leaning forward with her arms outstretched and her clothes billowing behind her, is considered by most to have been Eleanor Thornton, private secretary to and lover of John Walter Edward Douglas-Scott-Montagu, second Baron of Montagu of Beaulieu, an early motoring enthusiast and editor of *The Car Illustrated* magazine who was married to Lady Cecil Victoria Constance Kerr.

However, some, including the sculptor's daughter, think the model was more likely a composite of several women who posed for Sykes, although the facial features undoubtedly are Eleanor Thornton's. Thornton died in 1915 when the ship she was on, the *SS Persia*, sank after being torpedoed by a German U-boat near Crete while en route to India. Lord Montagu also was aboard the ship and initially was reported killed, but he survived after several days at sea in a lifeboat.

Within a few years, the Spirit of Ecstasy became standard equipment on all Rolls-Royces, and that continues to today. Over the years, due to changes in the design of vehicles and to the figure's placement on the radiator, there have been at least 11 versions of the Spirit of Ecstasy. In one version, used from 1934 to 1939 and from 1946 to 1955, the figure is kneeling. Today's standing version, from the 2003 BMW/Rolls-Royce Phantom model onward, is 3 inches high and, for reasons of safety, is mounted on a spring-loaded mechanism designed to retract instantly into the radiator shell if struck from any direction or if disturbed by a would-be thief. Also to deter theft, the Flying Lady can be retracted by pushing a button inside the car.

The standard Spirit of Ecstasy used today is made of polished stainless steel, although options include one of stainless steel with partial gold plating and one of illuminated crystal.

The Flying Lady is nearly as well known as the intertwined Rs of the Rolls-Royce logo.

Bentley's "Winged B" symbol, of which there have been many versions over the years, may not be quite as famous as the twin Rs or the Spirit of

Ecstasy, but from the first Bentley cars produced in 1921, the brand has been known for its fast, reliable and sporty vehicles. Today, as a unit of Volkswagen AG, Bentley sales exceed those of Rolls-Royce, which as noted is now owned by BMW AG.

This Rolls-Royce is all ready for a picnic   Photo by Sheila M. Lambert

Who Owns Rolls-Royce and Bentley Cars?

To generalize, there are two very different groups of people who own Rolls-Royce and Bentley cars: those who own (or lease) late-model cars, and those who own classic cars.

Owners of new or late model Rolls and Bentleys tend to be highly successful business owners, professionals or media, entertainment or sports personalities.

Queen Latifah, shown here at a 2009 event, is the owner of a late model Rolls-Royce

Late-model Roll-Royce owners (sometimes called "Rollers") include TV and movie personalities Queen Latifah, Jamie Foxx, Kim Kardashian, Khloe Kardashian, Mike Epps and Simon Cowell; singers Jennifer Lopez, Lady Gaga, Gwen Stefani, Rod Stewart, Brian Johnson, Elton John and Justin Bieber; rappers Big Boi, 50 Cent, Don Rocko, Cee-Lo, Rick Ross, Ray J, Tyga,

Sean Combs, Ice-T, Ludacris, Ne-Yo Green, Meek Mill, T.I., Waka Floka Flame, French Montana, Fat Joe, The Game, Yo Gotti and T-Pain; sports figures Tom Brady, Shaq O'Neal, David Beckham, Carlos Boozer, Lamar Odom, Joe Haden, Floyd Mayweather, Bruce Jenner, Reggie Bush, Kris Humphries, Tito Ortiz, Hanley Ramirez, Glenn Dorsey, Frank Gore, Francisco Cordero and Al Harrington.

Shaq O'Neal, shown here when he was with the Miami Heat, has owned both modern Bentley and Rolls-Royce cars Photo by Keith Allison

On the Bentley side, owners include sports figures Shaq O'Neal, Kobe Bryant, Lance Stephenson, Mike Comrie, Floyd Mayweather, Eljero Elia, Derrick Rose, Dwight Howard and Carlos Silva; rappers Jay Z, Ludacris Fabolous, The Game, Xzibit, Meek Mill, Lil' Twist, T.I., Soulja Boy; singers Jennifer Lopez, Cher, Mel B and Elton John; celebrities James Caan, Paris Hilton, Mark Wahlberg, Sharon and Ozzy Osbourne, Kim Kardashian, Simon Cowell, Christina Milian, Sylvester Stallone and Arnold Schwarzenegger.

You'll note that quite of few of these celebrities own both a Rolls-Royce and a Bentley, and a few own several of each.

The majority of late-model Rolls-Royce and Bentley drivers lease rather than buy their vehicles, usually through their business or professional corporations or partnerships. The ownership costs of these luxury vehicles are treated as business expenses and taken, as permitted, as a tax deduction.

Aside from flash-driven rappers and reality TV figures, the drivers typically are middle-aged, male and in the prime of their financial life. The average Bentley owner has an investible net worth of at least $5 million, according to research studies. After all, new Rolls-Royces or Bentleys cost up to half a million dollars or lease for $2,500 to $5,000 or more a month.

In 2014, sales of new Rolls-Royces totaled 4,063 worldwide, an all-time record. Bentley also had record sales in 2014, with 11,020 new Bentleys sold. Sales figures include cars that are leased.

On the other hand, those who have older, vintage or classic vehicles tend to own rather than lease them. Surveys of owners' and enthusiasts' club members suggest that these people skew heavily to older age groups, with at least a college degree, affluent but not necessarily wealthy. They are overwhelmingly male.

One study showed that about two-thirds of these vintage Bentley and Rolls-Royce enthusiasts were 60 or older, more than 90% were male and 80% were college grads with about one-fourth holding doctorates or other tertiary degrees. Nearly eight in 10 earned at least $100,000 a year, with three in 10 earning $250,000 or more.

By a slight margin, the most popular vehicles for this group are Rolls and Bentleys from the immediate post-World War II to mid-1960s, especially the Silver Cloud and Bentley S-Series, followed by "modern" vehicles (the Silver Shadow and Silver Spirit series) from the 1970s to 1990s.

The vintage-car owners like to tinker with their cars, and about three-fourths do at least some of the maintenance and restoration of their vehicles.

BUY A CLASSIC ROLLS-ROYCE OR BENTLEY

Although Rolls-Royce and Bentley were essentially the same motorcar from the early 1930s through the 1970s, with the main differences being that a Bentley had a different insignia, different grill and in some cases a slightly modified engine, Rolls-Royce and Bentley drivers see themselves differently. It may be a stereotype, but there is a lot of truth in this stereotype, that Rolls-Royce owners are more traditional and more establishment-oriented, while Bentley owners see themselves as more adventurous and sportier.

Some of the best known vintage and classic Rolls-Royce and Bentley owners include the late Vidal Sassoon, who owned a 1975 Silver Shadow; author Anne Rice who for a time had a 1977 Silver Wraith II; John Travolta, who has a 1979 Rolls-Royce Silver Shadow II and singer Beyoncé, who drives a gorgeous 1959 Silver Cloud II convertible, a gift from Jay-Z.

Comedian and car collector Jay Leno has a Silver Spur Limousine reportedly worth more than $10 million, a 1989 Bentley Turbo R and a 1930 Bentley GJ 400 with a huge 27-liter Rolls-Royce Merlin aircraft engine. Elvis Presley had several Rolls-Royce cars, including a 1966 Silver Cloud III and a 1960 Phantom V. Beatle John Lennon bought a 1965 Phantom V, which he later had painted in psychedelic colors.

Some of the most famous Rolls-Royces and Bentleys are those that appear in fiction. Travis McGee, the "salvage consultant" who appeared in 21 novels by John D. MacDonald in the 1960s to 1980s, drove a 1936 neon-blue Rolls-Royce, "Miss Agnes," that a previous owner had converted to a pickup truck. The exact model is never specified, except that McGee says it is "big" and "cruises easily at 80 mph." It could be the Phantom III or a 25/30, but after dumping it in a Florida canal McGee put in a 1972 Lincoln V-8 engine, transmission, power steering, air-conditioning and a Dodge suspension.

The most famous Bentley driver in the world of fiction is probably 007. Although in the movies Ian Fleming's James Bond famously drove an Aston Martin, Bond also had both a Bentley Mark VI and a 4½-litre Bentley Blower in *Moonraker*. He also drove 1930s-era Bentleys in *Casino Royale* and *Live and Let Die*. In *Thunderball*, 007 drove a Bentley R-Type coupé, converted to a two-seater convertible by H. J. Mulliner.

A website, the Internet Movie Cars Database (www.imcdb.org) devotes scores of pages to Rolls-Royce and Bentley cars that have appeared in films and television shows, listed by model and the extent to which they are featured in each movie or program. The Silver Shadow I appears in more movies and TV shows (a total of 467) than any other model.

One of the films to feature a Rolls-Royce most prominently is *The Yellow Rolls-Royce,* a 1964 movie written by Terry Rattigan and directed by Anthony Asquith. It has an all-star cast that includes Ingrid Bergman, Rex Harrison, Shirley MacLaine, Omar Shariff, George C. Scott, Art Carney, Jeanne Moreau and Alain Delon. Set in England, Italy and Yugoslavia in the years before and during the early course of World War II, the movie follows three consecutive owners of a 1930 Phantom II – an English aristocrat, a Miami gangster and a wealthy American widow. One of the 10 top-grossing films of 1964, *The New York Times* said it was a "pretty slick vehicle, that is pleasing to the eye and occasionally amusing, but it hardly seems worthy of all the effort and the noted personalities involved."

Factors to Consider Before Buying

In the end, which Rolls-Royce or Bentley motorcar you decide to buy, if any, comes down to your personal interests and preferences, the opinion of your spouse or partners and your budget.

A primary consideration definitely is budget, including the selling price of the vehicle, resale value and the likely initial and long-term costs of restoration, repairs and maintenance. Hard data on current prices of modern and vintage Rolls-Royces and Bentleys are presented in the chapter following.

A related consideration is the relative rarity of the model you are considering, taking in account the number produced and the number believed to still be in existence. Some models, such as the Rolls-Royce Phantom IV limousine, of which only 18 were produced from 1950 to 1956, and delivered almost entirely to heads of state and royalty, are of such rarity that they have great value to collectors, typically selling for over $1 million. The same is true, if to a lesser extent, with other Phantom models, some Bentleys such as the pre-World War II Mark V and some Rolls-Royce drophead (convertible) coupés.

It goes without saying that the very early Royce and Rolls-Royce cars made in Manchester before the opening of the Derby factory, have great historical value not only to collectors but also to museums. A 1904 10 horsepower two-seater, for example, went for more than $7 million at a Bonhams auction in London.

Early Silver Ghosts also are highly sought-after by collectors and can fetch large sums. A total of 7,876 of these were produced from 1907 to 1926. A 1912 Silver Ghost sold for $1.7 million at a Sotheby's auction in 1993, and more recently a different 1912 Silver Ghost sold for $7.1 million at auction. A Silver Ghost originally ordered in 1907 by Rolls-Royce's managing director, Claude Johnson as a company demonstrator, now owned by Bentley Motors Ltd., reportedly is insured for $35 million.

Some of the early "small" Rolls-Royces, such as the Twenty and 20/25, of which a total of 6,767 were produced between 1922 and 1936, while not inexpensive are more affordable for collectors, with many still on the road. That also goes for the first Phantoms, I and II, of which 5,220 were delivered between 1925 and 1933.

Of course, condition of the vehicle, the degree and quality of restoration if any, mileage, the original owner of the car and its particular history also play important roles in the value of the car.

But cars such as those noted above are in an elite level of their own. On a more practical level, unless you are independently wealthy, you likely will be looking at less exclusive and, typically, more modern cars. It is worth keeping in mind the production output of various models. The number of cars manufactured often also plays a role in the availability of parts.

Here are production runs of selected post-World War II models (the years are in most cases the model years):

Rolls-Royce Silver Shadow I, in production from 1965 to 1977: 20,603
Rolls-Royce Silver Shadow II, 1977-1980: 8,425
Rolls-Royce Silver Spirit, 1980-1989: 8,129
Bentley Turbo R, 1985-1997: 7,230
Rolls-Royce Silver Spur, 1980-1989: 6,238
Bentley Mark VI, 1946-1955: 5,201
Rolls-Royce Corniche (two-door hardtop and convertible): 4,329
Bentley S1, 1955-1959: 3,206
Rolls-Royce Silver Cloud III, 1959-1962: 2,809
Rolls-Royce Silver Cloud II, 1962-1966: 2,717
Bentley R-Type (including Continentals), 1946-1955: 2,528
Rolls-Royce Silver Cloud I, 1955-1959: 2,238
Rolls-Royce Silver Spur II, 1990-1993: 1,658
Rolls-Royce Silver Spirit II, 1990-1993: 1,152
Rolls-Royce New Silver Spur, 1996-2000: 802

Note that different sources may provide slightly different production numbers.

As to modern "21st century" vehicles, the BMW/Rolls-Royce cars from 2003 to the present, and the VW/Bentley cars, are when new, even leased, out of the reach of most except "the 1%." These uberluxury vehicles when new have prices of from around $200,000 to more than $500,000.

However, these cars depreciate very steeply and very rapidly. Within a few years, their value may drop by 50% to 60% or more from new. With their German engineering and modern safety and driving features, low-mileage pre-owned versions of these cars, especially Bentley models, may be more affordable than you think.

When thinking about which model is right for you, you also need to wrestle with these questions:

Are you planning to use the car as a "daily driver" or just for occasional use?

Do you expect to buy a collectible car as an investment, or are you just looking to get into a Rolls or Bentley at a price similar to, or less than, what you would pay for an ordinary used car? In the latter case generally you may expect some continued depreciation in the value.

Are you considering a veteran, vintage or classic model? Although the terms vary considerably in their use, generally a veteran vehicle is considered one built before World War I; a vintage is one built from World War I to World War II and sometimes in common usage through the 1940s or later; a classic is often considered to be a quality vehicle that is at least 20 years old and sometimes 25 or 30 or more. In the U.S., state motor vehicles departments generally consider vehicles to be "antiques" if they are 25 to 35 years old, the exact age varying from state to state.

Do you have a good understanding of the post-purchase costs – rehabilitation, rebuilding and restoration, repairs and ongoing maintenance costs? Even with a relatively modern Rolls-Royce or Bentley, as discussed elsewhere, in the early period of ownership you may pay as much or more in restoration, repairs and maintenance costs as you paid for the car itself. This of course varies greatly depending on whether you have the skills and time to do the work yourself, or whether you have to pay a factory-certified mechanic or high-quality restoration service at charges of $100 to $150 an hour, or more, plus very expensive parts.

Is a repair facility, either a dealership or an independent garage, within a reasonable distance? Just because there is a Rolls-Royce or Bentley dealership nearby, this does not necessarily mean that the dealership will work on your particular vehicle. For example, many Rolls-Royce dealerships only service 2003 and later cars built by BMW, and some private mechanics specialize in working only on Rolls-Royce or Bentley vehicles of certain types or ages. To some degree, the importance of this depends on how much of the restoration, repair and maintenance work on your vehicle you plan to do yourself. As many as three-fourths of the owners of older and vintage Rolls-Royces and Bentleys do at least some of the work on their own vehicles.

To what degree do you expect modern safety and comfort features? Automatic transmissions were not generally available in Rolls-Royces and Bentleys until 1952; power steering became available in 1956; air-conditioning also was introduced as an option in 1956, but further improvements were needed in later years; electric windows became available in 1959; power seats were introduced in 1965 and memory seats in the 1990 model year; anti-locking brakes (ABS) were introduced in 1987 and more widely in 1989; fuel injection was introduced in the Silver Spirit line in 1980, first in just export models and later for all models; remote-controlled anti-theft alarms and driver-side airbags were offered from 1989; passenger airbags from 1993; adjustable steering wheels from 1996.

Remember, as you move from older and simpler mechanics and engineering to more modern designs, the vehicles become more complex, more difficult to work on and often more expensive to repair.

Are you considering a right-hand or left-hand drive model, or both?

Are you cognizant of known problems with certain models, such as rusting of steel body panels in models from the early post-World War II period; broken crankshafts in some early V-8 engines; brake line and bushing leaks in 1980 and later models; electronics issues in the more complex vehicles built from 1980 on?

Pricing Rules of Thumb

While factors such as rarity, condition, demand by collectors and general economic conditions are almost always paramount in determining the price of a used Rolls-Royce or Bentley, there are some rough rules of thumb that typically apply across the board to the pricing equation. Among these are the following (but keep in mind that there are many exceptions to these rules):

Even though for much of the mid- to late-20th century, Rolls-Royce and Bentley cars of the same period were essentially the same vehicle, just with a different grill and badge, Rolls-Royce usually enjoys a pricing premium over Bentleys, typically of 5 to 10%, although in periods where few Bentleys were produced, their rarity value comes into play.

Long-wheelbase vehicles tend to sell for more than regular- or short-wheelbase models of the same period, all other things being equal.

Cars with a division between front and back seats are more sought-after, often fetching 10% to 20% or more than those without a division.

Coachbuilt vehicles, especially those of rarity or especially appealing design from the top coachbuilders such as Hooper, James Young, H. J. Mulliner, Park Ward and others, generally bring more than those using standard pressed steel bodies to produce "complete cars."

Two-door coupes (or coupés) bring a higher price than four-door saloons/sedans.

Convertibles (drophead coupés) are more sought-after and more expensive than the regular coupe version of the same model – you can easily see this in Corniche models.

True limousines – stretch models with acres of back seat space – are a niche vehicle sold to senior government officials and royalty, and today often used by limousine services or luxury hotels. They were produced in relatively low numbers and thus have rarity value. They typically bring a large premium over the saloon version of the same model, though few individual owners will want a colossal limousine for daily use.

Due in part to taxes and other government charges that must be included in the sales price, in general vehicles sold in Britain cost more than the same vehicle sold in the U.S. or Canada.

Low-mileage vehicles are more desirable than those with high-mileage, and thus bring more on the market, but there are exceptions. A low-mileage vehicle may have sat in a garage and have never been started for years, or it may have been used by only for occasional short trips around town, allowing rust and carbon build-up in the engine, requiring an expensive rebuild.

Vehicles with a "paper trail" for their service history, preferably with an authorized dealer, are more desirable than those without extensive service records, and thus bring a higher price.

With the exception of a few very rare cars, condition is perhaps the most important determinant of value for a specific year and model. A vehicle in *concours* or near-showroom condition may sell for five times as much as the same year and model in fair or even good condition, and it may go for 10 times or more as a vehicle in poor condition.

Cars that have been garaged since new generally look better than those that have not and thus usually are priced higher. Likewise, cars that have kept in temperate climates typically are more desirable than those that have been baked in the sun in tropical or semi-tropical climes, or vehicles from cold, snowy areas where a lot of salt is used on roadways, thus subjecting the car to rust. Rusted vehicles can be horribly expensive to repair and restore.

Used vehicles with one or only a few owners are more desirable than those with many owners. The fewer owners, the better. The worst situation is where a vehicle has many owners, perhaps a dozen or more, with most owning for only a few months. This typically indicates that the vehicle has serious, perhaps hidden, mechanical or other problems that the owners do not want to pay to have fixed.

With exceptions that go to prove the rule, generally sales prices of later model used Rolls-Royces and Bentleys (from 1965 onwards) are flat to only slightly appreciating. Buyers do not yet see the Silver Shadow (1965-1980) and Silver Spirit/Spur (1980-1998) series as true collectors' items and thus generally these vehicles are not appreciating much in value. There are exceptions, of course, for rare models or those in superb condition.

Most earlier models are appreciating, up to and including the Silver Cloud. The Silver Cloud III is in particular vogue now. However, in most cases appreciation is not nearly to the extent of highly collectible models of Ferrari, Bugatti and other exotic cars.

Classic car prices are subject to the same economic cycles as most other commodities. For example, there was a general downturn in prices for classic and collectible cars that began with the severe global recession in 2008. Prices hit their nadir in 2010 and 2011, after which they began to climb again. In all but a few cases, current prices for most classes of collectible cars are at or near their all-time high.

The classic car market has fads and trends just as do many other product categories. For example, the American "muscle car" fad peaked in 2007, and prices have yet to completely regain levels seen in that year. More modest fads are seen in the Rolls-Royce and Bentley collectible market. Currently, Silver Clouds are enjoying strong demand, and the rather unusual Silver Seraph, built at Crewe by Volkswagen but with a BMW engine also seem to be experiencing a mini-fad.

Obviously, a clear title is a necessity. Often the lowest-priced Rolls-Royce and Bentley vehicles, ones that are offered for a few thousands dollars on eBay or elsewhere, have only salvage titles, indicating in most cases that the vehicle was written off as a total loss by an insurance company due to a wreck or had serious flood damage. CarFax (www.carfax.com) is a leading company that provides a title history based on Vehicle Identification Number. Reports include information on registration, odometer readings, accident and major repair history including frame and structural damage, airbag deployment and usage of the vehicle as a taxi or rental car. Some CarFax report information is available at no charge, while a complete report on up to five vehicles might cost around $40.

Twelve Steps to Buying a Rolls-Royce or Bentley

Step 1: If you haven't already done so, familiarize yourself with the history of Rolls-Royce and Bentley and with the various models manufactured since 1906, when Rolls-Royce was founded. The best way to do this is through reading, or at least scanning, books like this one and those listed in the Bibliography section. Many of the books are lavishly illustrated with photographs of the different models and series. You'll probably need to spend at least $100 for several enthusiast books, most likely used, and you could spend a lot more, but it's a sound investment in education.

Step 2: Decide, if you can, why you want to own a Rolls-Royce or Bentley – as a car to drive regularly or only occasionally, as a restoration project for your retirement or leisure time, as a hobby allowing you to meet and get to know other enthusiasts, as a possible appreciating asset or for some other reason. Recognize that with ownership comes responsibility -- for the care, maintenance, storage and possible resale of these rare vehicles.

Step 3: Decide, if you can, in which model or models you are most interested. Perhaps you are interested in "modern" Rolls-Royce and Bentley cars, those from the Silver Shadow/T-Series and later, or you admire the iconic look of the Silver Cloud and Bentley S-Series vehicles, or you want an earlier "small horsepower" vehicle. At the very least, decide whether you want a Rolls-Royce or a Bentley, or if it doesn't matter. True, for much of their history the two motorcars were built by the same company shared almost everything except their badges and radiator grills, but even so the two cars have quite different "images" and in many cases appeal to different types of people.

Step 4: Join one of the owners' or enthusiasts' clubs. The two largest clubs are the Rolls-Royce Owners' Club (**RROC**), based in and focused mainly on the United States, and the Rolls-Royce Enthusiasts' Club (**RREC**), based in England and focused mainly on the United Kingdom and Europe. *See the chapter on enthusiasts' club for detailed information on these organizations.* Both clubs, despite their names, are devoted to Bentley as well as Rolls-Royce. Both gladly accept members who have an interest in these motorcars, whether or not they actually own one. Both offer a wealth of information for members, with extensive websites, forums and magazines. You also will have the opportunity to meet other members at local, regional, national and international gatherings. Just as important, you will be able to see many fine examples of Rolls-Royce and Bentley cars, and you will hear and read many "war stories" about buying, owning, repairing, restoring and maintaining these cars. Membership may cost you a couple of hundred dollars a year, but again, this modest investment will provide an invaluable education. Several active members of RROC and RREC have written about purchasing a used Rolls-Royce or Bentley. In particular, you may want to look at the article, "How to Buy a Rolls-Royce or Bentley" on the RROC website by R. Pierce Reid, co-owner of The Vintage Garage in Vermont, and the RROC forum post "Buying a Used Rolls-Royce or Bentley" by John Robison, of JE Robison Service in Springfield, Mass. Both are technical consultants for RROC.

Step 5: Decide on a budget for your purchase. This budget should include not only the purchase price but also the likely cost of repairs or restoration over the course of the first year or so of ownership. The latter can sometimes exceed the former. Valuation guides such as *Hagerty Price Guide* are useful in giving you an idea of current prices of most models, at various condition levels, but at best these guides are only a starting point. You should also put a figure on the likely operating costs of your vehicle once it is in the driving condition you desire. Most of these luxury vehicles get very poor gas mileage by today's standards, typically just 10 to 15 miles per U.S. gallon. Later models generally require premium fuel and pricey specialized fluids. Regular maintenance, especially if you have it done at an authorized dealer or a highly trained specialist, can be very expensive. A trained and experienced Rolls-Royce or Bentley mechanic at an authorized dealership or specialized service center typically will get $100 to $150 an hour, and new parts are wildly expensive.

Step 6: Determine where you will have your car serviced. Your local imported car repair shop likely can't or won't work on a Bentley or Rolls-Royce. Is there a trained and respected Rolls-Royce/Bentley specialist or authorized dealer in your area? If not, how far are you willing to drive or trailer your vehicle for service? Keep in mind that even if there is a Rolls-Royce or

Bentley dealership in your city, or a garage specializing in these cars, that's no guarantee that they will work on your particular model. As noted elsewhere, a lot of Rolls-Royce dealers now only work on models manufactured from 2003, when BMW took over the brand. Other specialists will not work on vehicles older than a certain year, or they may concentrate on only certain models, such as cars manufactured from 1955. Unless you are capable of and expert enough to do most of the work on your car yourself, your trained and experienced Rolls-Royce or Bentley mechanic will be the best friend of your car.

Step 7: See as many Bentley and Rolls-Royce cars for sale as you can. It is a bit like looking at existing homes. A few days of touring homes for sale and attending open houses will make you an "instant expert" on home values, at least in that specific area. See cars for sale advertised locally, even if you have no real interest in the particular model advertised. Being local, it will only take a brief bit of your time. Attend auctions. Look through ads in enthusiasts' club magazines. Spend time looking closely at ads in car websites that offer classic cars for sale, such as Hemmings.com, ClassicCars.com, AutoTrader.com, eBay.com, VintageDrivingMachines.com and others.

Step 8: When you find a vehicle that could be one that you want to own, whether it is being sold by a dealer or by an individual, go see the car. Assuming you're serious about the vehicle, even if it requires an expensive trip by air you owe it to yourself to see the car in person. Spend as much time with it as you can. Take it for a test drive of at least 30 minutes, in a variety of conditions -- highway, city, traffic, etc. (This likely will not be possible if you are buying at auction.) Check the CarFax or other vehicle history record, to be sure the title is clean, that the mileage claimed is accurate and that the vehicle has not been in a serious accident. Try to meet in person with the owner or immediate former owner in the case of a vehicle being sold by a dealer or at auction. Ask every question you can think of about the car, its service history and its problems. Try to see the service records and go through them carefully, asking questions. You can tell a lot about the car from its owner. For example, is he or she a member of an enthusiasts' club? Does he or she seem to know and love cars? What other cars does he or she have, and what condition are they in? What's your gut feeling about the owner/former owner as a person?

Step 9: Have the car inspected carefully by a competent, trained Rolls-Royce or Bentley mechanic. Yes, this may be difficult to do, unless the vehicle for sale is located near a reputable dealership or Rolls-Royce/Bentley specialist. And, yes, since you will likely pay $100 to $150 an hour for the inspection, it will be expensive. The cheaper inspection services offered through classic car and general car sales websites can be somewhat helpful, but these inspectors are not expert in Rolls-Royce or Bentley cars. A few hundred dollars spent now could save your tens of thousands of dollars and many headaches in the future. Try to have every major area – engine, transmission, brakes, suspension, air-conditioning, electronics, leather, woodwork, paint and others – checked thoroughly. If possible, get the mechanic to put in writing all defects found and a rough estimate of the expected cost to have them put in order.

Step 10: Before getting to final negotiation, take care of the details. Are you sure the seller has clear, unencumbered title to the vehicle? How will the title transfer be accomplished? Remember, rules and costs vary considerably country by country and state by state. Talk to your insurance agent to discuss insurance costs, or arrange special classic car insurance. If you are having the car trailered or otherwise shipped to your home, work out the details carefully. Are you sure that the big motorcar will fit in your garage, and if not where will you keep it? Can you get a custom cover for it? How will you protect it from the elements and from nature? Mice are the bane of many owners' existence, as once they nest in a vehicle it can be nearly impossible to eliminate their mess and smell short of a totally replacing the interior.

Step 11: Negotiate the sale, whether buying from a dealer or an individual. Remember, the asking price is just that. It is the top price the seller hopes to get. Almost in every case, the seller will take less, perhaps 10 to 25% less than the initial asking price. If you have found a car you love you may be ready just to pay the asking price and take your Rolls-Royce or Bentley home, but as a willing and able buyer you are in the driver's seat. As with real estate, it is usually much easier to buy than to sell.

Step 12: If you complete the deal, take the car home. Spend the money necessary to get the car in tip-top condition. Then drive it and enjoy it!

How Much Will You Pay?

Using our database of hundreds of Rolls-Royce and Bentley motorcars offered for sale in 2015, here are price ranges and median prices (the price midway between lowest and highest) for selected models. Some rare models have too few offerings to provide meaningful data, and some other models listed have only limited data, typically fewer than 20 of the model offered for sale.

Keep these facts in mind:

Data presented here are from published asking prices, obtained from automobile websites such as Hemming's, eBay Motors, ClassicCars.com, AutoTrader.com, JamesEdition.com, VintageDrivingMachines.com and others. In addition, asking prices are also comprised from for-sale advertisements in publications of the Rolls-Royce Owners' Club and Rolls-Royce Enthusiasts' Club and other classic car clubs. Information is also compiled with a view to results at auto auction sites. It also includes a review of current prices from classic car valuation companies including Hagerty and, to the degree available (some online valuation sites report on cars only from the early 1990s and later) from online car valuation sites such as NADA and Kelley Blue Book.

Again, prices shown generally are *asking prices*. We have reviewed published sales prices from auction sites and individual sales, and from classic car valuation companies, but such information is limited, as in many cases actual sales prices are kept confidential between buyer and seller, or the prices published are suspect.

The difference between asking price and selling price varies depending on economic conditions, demand for the particular model, condition of the vehicle and of course the economic circumstances and bargaining abilities of the buyer and seller. In general, luxury vehicles such as Bentley and Rolls-Royce end up selling for from 10 to 25% lower than the original asking price, but this difference can vary greatly in any individual situation.

At any given time, about three-fourths of these vehicles advertised for sale are offered by dealers, either used car dealers or the used car division of new car dealers, or at auto auctions. The rest are offered by individual sellers.

Price range and median asking price data from out database are shown without regard to condition of the vehicle. A separate line item, Valuation

BUY A CLASSIC ROLLS-ROYCE OR BENTLEY

Considering Condition, takes into account the cosmetic and mechanical condition of some, not all, models of vehicles, as described below.

The Valuation Considering Condition (shown for some models only) shown is from our own database, cross-referenced with various published price valuation guides. It reflects five condition categories: Poor, Fair, Good, Excellent and *Concours*. Keep in mind that these categories are to some degree subjective, and buyers and sellers may disagree on the category.

Poor means that the vehicle is not drivable without significant repairs, may not be running and may have a salvage title.

Fair means that the vehicle has visible flaws such as paint chipping, scratches on chrome or stainless work or cracked or split leather seats. It is in running condition but may require a number of repairs and possibly complete restoration.

Good means that the vehicle drives and runs well, though it typically is not used for daily transportation. Some cosmetic defects may be present, but not as many or as serious as in Poor and Fair categories.

Excellent means that the vehicle looks in near show-room condition, and any minor flaws or mechanical problems would only appear on a close inspection. This vehicle may have been restored but may have slipped slightly due to age or being driven regularly.

Concours applies only to vehicles that are among the best in the world in their class and are capable of winning their category even at major show events. Most have undergone total restoration or have been carefully maintained since new in like-new condition.

A majority of vehicles on the market will fall in the Fair to Good categories, with a sizeable number of sellers claiming Excellent condition. *Concours* condition is rare.

Note that due to part of the sourcing of the Valuation Considering Condition, from auction results and insurance valuation guides, the Valuation Considering Condition reflects actual sales prices than does the median and mean price, which reflect primarily asking prices.

No warranty is offered or implied for this information. Please use it as a general guide only. For more detailed model-by-model and year-by-year information, especially on post-World War II vehicles, see the *Hagerty Price Guide* or other classic car price guides. Kelley Blue Book, Edmunds, NADA and similar online auto pricing guides unfortunately have only limited information on used Rolls-Royce and Bentley cars, especially those from before the early

1990s. Where information from these price guides is available, prices often reflect dealer asking prices and tend to be higher than the overall market.

Keep in mind that most of the prices show are for cars offered in the United States, Canada, the U.K. and Europe. Prices shown are in U.S. dollars, and fluctuating exchange rates can impact some of the valuations.

Further, the collector car market is dynamic, with changes occurring constantly. Prices shown here reflect market conditions in 2015. Because of the relatively small number of Rolls-Royce and Bentley cars manufactured – a total of fewer than 200,000 over more than a century – and the low number of vehicles of some models that are on the market at any given time, for some models the data are quite limited and thus subject to large fluctuations over time.

Again, where shown the median asking price is the point with one-half of the vehicles selling for less and the other one-half for more. Mean asking price is the average selling price of all models of the vehicle on the market. It is computed by adding the total value of all asking prices in our database and dividing by the number of vehicles for sale. Median, mean and Valuation Considering Condition are presented only for selected models. Most figures are rounded.

ROLLS-ROYCE
1906-1926 Rolls-Royce 40/50 (Silver Ghost)
Price Range: $159,000 to $2,000,000+
Median Asking Price: $395,000 (limited data)

1925-1941 Rolls-Royce Phantom I, II and III
Range: $105,000 to $240,000
Median Asking Price: $200,000 (limited data)

1929-1936 Rolls-Royce 20/25
Range: $19,000 to $283,000
Median Asking Price: $70,000 (limited data)

1935-1939 Rolls-Royce 25/30
Range: $55,000 to $170,000
Median Asking Price: $95,000 (limited data)

1946-1955 Rolls-Royce Silver Dawn

Range: $42,000 to $80,000
Median Asking Price: $55,000 (limited data)
Valuation Considering Condition:
Poor $15,000
Fair $30,000
Good $40,000
Excellent $45,000 to $65,000
Concours $58,000 to $85,000

1955-1965 Silver Cloud I, II and III

Range: $12,500 to $770,000 (database of 75 vehicles on market)
Median Asking Price: $73,900
Mean Asking Price: $119,650
Valuation Considering Condition (higher prices for Silver Cloud III and certain rare models):
Poor $20,000
Fair $35,000
Good $50,000
Excellent $60,000 to $100,000
Concours $65,000 to $175,000+

1965-1980 Silver Shadow I and II

Range: $4,000 to $62,000 (database of 102 vehicles on market)
Median Asking Price: $22,000
Mean Asking Price: $24,650
Valuation Considering Condition:
Poor $3,000
Fair $5,000
Good $12,000
Excellent $17,000 to $20,000
Concours $26,000 to $32,000

1972-1995 Rolls-Royce Corniche I, II and III

Range: $15,750 to $200,000 (database of 68 vehicles on market)
Median Asking Price: $62,900
Mean Asking Price: $66,745

Valuation Considering Condition:
Poor $15,000
Fair $25,000
Good $30,000
Excellent $55,000
Concours $58,000 to $75,000

The owner of this 1959 Phantom V with somewhat unusual body by Hooper reportedly was asking about $150,000 for it in 2015   Photo by Sheila M. Lambert

1959-1990 Rolls-Royce Phantom V and Phantom VI Limousine
Valuation Considering Condition:
Poor N/A
Fair $100,000
Good $120,000
Excellent $140,000
Concours $145,000 to $225,000+

1980-1989 Silver Spirit/Silver Spur and Others in SZ Series
Range: $5,775 to $49,900 (database of 142 vehicles on market)

Median Asking Price: $21,900
Mean Asking Price: $22,185
Valuation Considering Condition:
Poor $3,500
Fair $7,000
Good $15,000
Excellent $20,000
Concours $25,000 to $30,000

1989-1998 Silver Spirit/Spur II, III, IV and Others in SZ Series
Range: $13,000 to $66,500 (database of 81 vehicles on market)
Median Asking Price: $29,900
Mean Average Asking Price: $33,400
Valuation Considering Condition:
Poor $8,000
Fair $11,000
Good $18,000
Excellent $24,000
Concours $32,000 to $38,000

1998-2002 Silver Seraph (VW)
Range: $38,000 to $76,000
Median Asking Price: $53,000 (limited data)

2003-2014 Rolls-Royce Phantom (BMW)
Range: $150,000 to $360,000
Median Asking Price: $240,000 (used)

BENTLEY
1946-1952 Bentley Mark VI
Range: $9,750 to $210,000
Median Asking Price: $57,000 (limited data, varies greatly by year and style)
Mean Asking Price: $69,300
Valuation Considering Condition:
Poor $9,000
Fair $40,000
Good $25,000 to $82,000

Excellent $39,000 to $120,000
Concours $98,000 to $165,000

1955-1965 Bentley S-Series (excludes Continental models, which are much higher)
Range: $10,000 to $225,000
Median Asking Price: $58,000
Valuation Considering Condition:
Poor $15,000
Fair $22,000
Good $35,000 to $45,000
Excellent $43,000 to $45,000
Concours $68,000 to $100,000

1985-1997 Bentley Turbo R
Range: $10,000 to $52,000 (database of 41 vehicles on market)
Median Asking Price: $24,900
Mean Asking Price: $25,500
Valuation Considering Condition:
Poor $8,000
Fair $12,000
Good $19,000
Excellent $21,000-$23,000
Concours $26,000 to $30,000

2003-2014 Bentley (VW)
Range: $44,000 to $240,000
Median Asking Price: $89,000 (used)

Suggested Models for First-Time Buyers

In the end, the Rolls-Royce or Bentley motorcar you buy, or decide not to buy, is a personal decision. You may have an attachment to a particular model due to your family or personal history with the car, because a friend or romantic partner owned one, because someone you greatly admire had one, because it appeared in a favorite film, television show or book or simply because you've always admired the way it looks.

Having said that, except for the independently wealthy for whom money is no object, certain Rolls-Royce and Bentley vehicles are simply beyond the budget of most of us. For example, a museum-quality early Silver Ghost with unique histories might go for $1 to $2 million or more, and even an "ordinary" Silver Ghost is likely to sell for several hundred thousand dollars. An early 1960s Silver Cloud drophead (convertible) coupe in top condition could sell for $200,000 to $500,000 or more. The Phantom IV limousine, made in very small numbers and delivered mostly to royalty and heads of state, can fetch well over a million today, and Phantoms I, II, III, V and VI in excellent or *concours* condition usually are well into the six figures.

If budget isn't a concern, then go for the best of whichever Rolls or Bentley you've always wanted. For the rest of us, here are a few of the more realistic options for a used Rolls-Royce or Bentley, with the reasons why they are models to consider. Not everyone will agree with this list, and some would add other models to it.

1965-1980 Rolls-Royce Silver Shadow and Derivatives

Introduced in 1965 and in production in various forms until 1980, the Rolls-Royce Silver Shadow could be considered the first "modern" Rolls-Royce, with classic yet contemporary styling that did not become dated, a monocoque chassis (the body and chassis were integrated) and features such as V-8 engine, disc brakes, standard automatic transmission, air-conditioning and power steering. More than 37,000 Shadows were produced at Crewe during that time, making it the best-selling series in the entire history of Rolls-Royce. Altogether, including derivatives such as the Bentley T-Series, the Corniche and Camargue and the long wheelbase Silver Wraith II, some 40,000 vehicles were produced at Crewe during the Silver Shadow years.

Due to the popularity of the Silver Shadow and the large number on the market, the availability of replacement parts either after-market or from

Volkswagen-owned Bentley and also due its modern driving characteristics, it is one of the cars recommended as a "starter" model for the Rolls-Royce enthusiast. Having said that, there are a lot of badly maintained Shadows out there, and it's easy to buy a $15,000 Shadow that will cost you another $15,000 or more to get into dependable driving condition; after paying that you still have a car that is still likely only worth around $15,000.

Don't expect much if any appreciation on the typical Silver Shadow, at least not over the next decade or so.

1972 Silver Shadow long-wheelbase saloon in superb condition Photo by Sheila M. Lambert

Used Shadows are indeed relatively affordable, with a median asking price of around $22,000 today, with a range of $4,200 for a salvage vehicle to $60,000. The mean average asking price is $24,950. The median and mean averages presented here do not take into account condition. Valuation guides that purport to provide fair market value and that do factor in condition show a value range of from $5,000 for Shadows in Fair condition, $12,000 for Good, $17,000 to $20,000 for Excellent and $26,000 to $32,000 for *Concours* condition.

Low-mileage Silver Shadows in excellent condition and requiring fewer repairs are usually advertised in the high-$20,000 range. Actual selling price is more difficult to judge, but based on public auction and valuation guides selling prices would be from 10 to 25% lower than the asking price.

Keep in mind that dealers tend to have the highest asking price, often 15 to 25% or more than the asking price of owners, and that auctions generally result in the lowest selling price.

The equivalent in a Bentley is the T-Series, which is essentially the same vehicle as the Silver Shadow of similar manufacture date except for the badge and the radiator grill. This was a low point in Bentley's history, at least in terms of sales. Only 2,464 T-Series vehicles were built, including Corniche and Camargue editions. Because of their relative rarity, Bentleys produced during the Silver Shadow years often command more on the re-sale market.

The most significant changes in the Silver Shadow series came in 1976-1977, with the introduction of the Silver Shadow II and Bentley T2. At the same time, the long-wheelbase version of the Silver Shadow II was renamed the Silver Wraith II. Many small design changes were made over the years of production, along with evolutionary mechanical improvements. Of the mechanical changes in the Silver Shadow II and Silver Wraith II, probably the most important was the introduction of rack-and-pinion steering.

Facts and Stats

Here are some key facts about the Silver Shadow and its derivatives. Of course, over the course of the 15-year production run, many changes and improvements were made.

Engine: 6.2-liter (6,230 cc) V-8 with 16 valves, twin carburetors and output of 200 hp (1965-70) and 6.7 liter (6,750 cc) V-8 with 16 valves, twin carburetors and output of 220 hp (1970-1980)

Transmission: 3-speed automatic, sourced from General Motors (4-speed automatic in the U.K. 1965-1970)

Wheelbase: 119.5 inches (a long-wheelbase version at 123.5 inches was introduced in the U.S. in 1970 and called the Silver Wraith II from 1976)

Length: 203.5 inches

Weight: 4,648 lbs. (regular wheelbase)

Price when introduced in 1965: 6,557 British pounds (US$18,360 in 1965 dollars or US$138,000 in today's dollars); by 1980, the price had risen to 41,960 pounds (US$97,800 in 1980 dollars or US$281,000 in today's dollars)

Performance

Top Speed 115 mph

0-60 mph 10.9 seconds

Fuel Economy 12 mpg combined city/highway

Standard Features: 4-wheel disc brakes with hydraulic system licensed from Citröen, independent rear suspension, power-assisted steering, air-conditioning, rack-and-pinion steering (from 1976-77)

Pros and Cons of Silver Shadow
Pros:

Due to the large number built, there are lots of these vehicles on the market from which to choose

First "modern" Rolls-Royce with hydraulic disc brakes, dependable GM transmission, excellent air-conditioning system, long-lasting V-8 engine, good riding characteristics

Classic, stylish design

Median asking price as of 2015 is not unreasonable, but expect to pay more – in the high $20,000 range -- for quality, low-mileage vehicles in excellent condition ... if you can find one

Cons:

A surprising number, perhaps a majority, of Silver Shadows on the market today have not been adequately maintained, so repairs and rebuilding can cost as much or more than what you pay for car – a total restoration could be $30,000 to $100,000

Silver Shadows in top condition needing few repairs are surprisingly rare

Bottom of body panels, except doors, bonnet and boot, which are aluminum alloy, are susceptible to rust

Power windows, door locks and cruise control can be troublesome

CV joints in older Shadows may need rebuilding, a $5,000 job at a dealership

A few parts may be difficult to find and all new parts are extremely expensive

Hydraulic brake system needs careful maintenance, and brakes on cars that have not been driven regularly may rust and seize up

Older vehicles with poor maintenance may have interior leather and wood veneer issues, costly to redo

If the exterior paint has deteriorated, a factory-quality paint job can run $10,000+

Only modest appreciation is expected in the immediate future, although Shadows in excellent or better condition likely will see appreciation over the long-term

1980-1989 Rolls-Royce Silver Spirit and Derivatives

Another popular and widely available option for buyers is the 1980s Silver Spirit and its long wheelbase sibling, the Silver Spur. The Silver Spirit or SZ series replaced the popular Silver Shadow line, building on its success and adding significant refinements and improvements.

While total sales of the initial SZ series, around 14,000, didn't come close to matching production of the Shadow, the Spirits and Spurs of the 1980s proved very successful for Rolls-Royce, with sales averaging around 1,800 a year, and there are many fine examples still on the road today.

The Silver Spirit/Spur line was an evolution of the Shadow, both in terms of design and engineering, but many significant changes were introduced. The SZ series did retain the popular and proven 6.7-liter V-8 and the dependable GM-sourced three-speed automatic transmission. However, improvements in ride were evident in the Spirit, with an improved ride height control system and gas-charged shock absorbers. The hydraulic braking and ride damping system switched from standard brake fluid to the use of mineral oil.

Many of the SZs remain in essentially good condition, but some owners have deferred maintenance due to its high cost. These cars are relatively complicated, especially the hydraulic braking and ride damping systems. Electronics can also be a problem. Some of the vehicles develop rattles and squeaks.

In our database for 2015, the median asking price for 1980 through 1989 Silver Spirits and Silver Spurs is $21,900 and the mean asking price is $22,200, with the range being from a few thousand dollars for salvage title cars to around $50,000. Median selling price at auction sales, however, is only about $14,000. For the most expensive 1980s SZ cars, you'll get a very low mileage vehicle – probably under 30,000 miles -- in Excellent to *Concours* condition.

1985 Silver Spirit, shown here beside a classic 1950s Chevrolet

Facts and Stats

Here are some key facts about the 1980s-era Silver Spirit and its derivatives.

Engine:

6.7 liter (6,750 cc) V-8 with 16 valves, Bosch fuel injection (initially in North America only) and estimated output of 240 hp

Transmission: 3-speed GM 400 automatic

Wheelbase: 120 inches for Silver Spirit, 124 inches for Silver Spur

Length: 207 inches for Silver Spirit, 210 inches for Silver Spur (U.S. models were slightly longer due to bumpers required by U.S. regulators)

Weight: 4,949 lbs. Silver Spirit, 5010 pounds Silver Spur

Price when introduced in 1980: 49,629 British pounds (US$115,600 in 1980 dollars or US$322,100 in today's dollars) for Silver Spirit and 56,408 pounds for Silver Spur (US$131,400 in 1980 dollars or US$377,600 in today's dollars). Note: As the pound's value versus the dollar declined during the 1980s – it got as low as US$1.10 per pound briefly in 1985 and averaged $1.30 for the year – Americans enjoyed lower prices on British-made cars.

Performance

Top Speed 119 mph

0-60 mph 10.2 seconds

Fuel Economy 14 mpg

Standard Features: 4-wheel 11-inch disc brakes on 15-inch wheels with hydraulic braking and automatic leveling system using mineral oil, independent coil spring suspension front and rear, power-assisted steering, air-conditioning, power windows and door locks, catalytic converter, ABS braking from 1987

Pros and Cons of 1980s Silver Spirit/Silver Spur

Pros:

Improved ride and handling, with sophisticated braking, suspension and electronics systems

Reliable, proven V-8 engine and dependable GM transmission

Classic, stylish design, an update of the Silver Shadow series with the exterior changed only in minor details through the 1990s

Typically beautiful interior finishings, with wood veneers, Connolly leather and Wilson carpets

Median asking price is reasonable, but higher for quality, low-mileage vehicles

Cons:

Complicated wiring and hydraulic systems, daunting for anyone but a trained Rolls-Royce mechanic to work on

Repairs and new parts when needed are very expensive

Some parts may be difficult to find

Rattles and squeaks may appear in some of these cars as they age

Everflex roof used on many of these vehicles tends to give problems with age, including buckling and allowing moisture and rust under the fabric

Little appreciation expected in the immediate future, although cars in excellent or better condition likely will appreciate over the long-term

1989-1998 Rolls-Royce Silver Spirit II/Silver Spur II and Derivatives

In the fall of 1989, for the 1990 model year, Rolls-Royce introduced the second generation of the Silver Spirit series. Although many of the changes were minor, there were enough of them to warrant a name change, to Silver Spirit II and the long wheelbase Silver Spur II.

1991 Silver Spur II on Biltmore Estate in Asheville, NC – note Biltmore House, the largest private home in America on hill in background   Photo by Sheila M. Lambert

One of the biggest improvements was the adaptive damping ride system that automatically adjusted the ride firmness depending on road conditions and speed. This definitely improved the ride characteristics of the Silver Spirit line. Inside the car there were a number of changes and enhancements, including a new power seat adjustment with memory, a revised fascia layout and automatic release of the parking brake when Drive was selected. In late 1991, a new GM four-speed transmission replaced the dependable but now dated GM three-speed. Later in the 1990s, other upgrades, including passenger-side airbag and adjustable steering wheel, were introduced.

In late 1993, the II series gave way to the III series, and later to the IV series. To lessen the marketing confusion, names for the 1996 model year reverted just to Silver Spirit and Silver Spur. A limited number of 350 horsepower turbocharged vehicles, badged as Flying Spur, were produced, marking the first time Rolls-Royce used a turbocharged engine, although turbocharging had been offered on Bentley from the early 1980s. There also was a stretched Silver Spur Touring Limousine built for that specialized market.

For would-be Rolls-Royce owners, these 1990s-era vehicles are the last of "true" Rolls-Royces, built slowly, deliberately and mostly by hand at the Crewe factory. Although some of the engineering and even the design date back to the mid-1960s, these are the most modern British-made Rolls-Royces, for after this decade Rolls-Royce would be owned briefly by Volkswagen and then by BMW. Although the BMW-era Rolls-Royces, with their BMW engines and glitzy designs, may be more dependable they will never be classics in the sense of the Crewe-built Rolls-Royces.

The 1990s-era Silver Spirit/Spur series is now 25 years old. Typically they are priced higher than the 1980s Spirits/Spurs but are still relatively affordable. Our database of cars for sale from this period shows a median asking price of around $29,900 and mean average of $33,400. Actual sales prices are often 10 to 20 or 25% lower, depending on the financial needs of the seller. For not much more than the price of a late-model Toyota Camry, you can buy a 1990s Spirit/Spur with 20,000 to 70,000 miles on it, in Good to Excellent condition.

However, the complexity of these vehicles can mean high costs for repairs, and even for a seemingly well-maintained model you may need to quickly spend $5,000 to $15,000 or more to repair nagging problems such as leaking brake systems, bad bushings, air conditioning problems, electronics glitches and other defects. For vehicles with cosmetic issues inside or out, the cost of restoring the appearance to original quality will stun you.

Facts and Stats

Here are some key facts about the 1990s-era Silver Spirit and its derivatives.

Engine:

6.7 liter (6,750 cc) V-8 with 16 valves, fuel injection with estimated output of 250 hp

Transmission: 4-speed GM automatic (after 1991)

Wheelbase: 120 inches for Silver Spirit II, 124 inches for Silver Spur II and later

Length: 207 inches for Silver Spirit II, 210 inches for Silver Spur II and later

Weight: 4,949 lbs. Silver Spirit II, 5,010 lbs. Silver Spur II

Price when introduced in fall 1989 for 1990 model year:

85,609 British pounds (US$140,400 in 1989 dollars or US$268,000 in today's dollars) for Silver Spirit II and 99,758 pounds for Silver Spur II (US$163,600 in 1989 dollars or US$312,300 in today's dollars)

Performance

Top Speed 126 mph for 1989-92, 134 mph for later vehicles

0-60 mph 10 seconds

Fuel Economy 14.5 mpg (up to 17 mpg on III series and later vehicles)

Standard Features: 6.7-liter V-8 fuel-injected engine, automatic transmission sourced from GM (4-speed from 1992 model year), enhanced automatic adaptive damping suspension system, rack-and-pinion steering, four-wheel disc brakes with hydraulic braking and self-leveling system using mineral oil, ABS system, 15-inch alloy wheels, updated fascia, two-level air-conditioning and heating system, leather-covered steering wheel instead of former Bakelite wheel, power steering, power windows, power front seats with memory (also, power adjustable rear seats in Silver Spur II), remote door opener and alarm system, driver airbag, passenger airbag from 1993

Pros and Cons of 1990s Silver Spirit/Silver Spur Series

Pros:

Last of the "true" Rolls-Royces built mostly by hand at Crewe

Improved ride and handling, with complex but sophisticated braking, suspension and electronics systems

Classic, stylish design, updated for the 1990s

Typically beautiful interior finishings, with wood veneers, Connolly leather and Wilson carpets

Median asking price of around $29,900, and a mean average of listings for sale in 2015 of $33,400, reflects the above-average condition of many offerings, and selling price is frequently significantly less; many cars available for $15,000 to $22,000 or less, but expect to pay considerably more for high-quality, low-mileage vehicles in Excellent or better condition

Cons:

Extremely complicated wiring and hydraulic systems, daunting for anyone but a trained Rolls-Royce mechanic to work on

Repairs when needed are extremely expensive

A few parts may be difficult to find

Everflex roofs may allow moisture build-up and rust on the steel roof, and exposure to sun may cause buckling

V-8 engine, while reliable, has engineering that dates back some five decades and was much in need of a total redesign

Front seat room may be less than ideal for tall or large drivers, especially in early 1990s models without adjustable steering wheel

Little appreciation expected in the immediate future, although cars in excellent or better condition likely will appreciate over the long-term

1965 Silver Cloud III   Photo by Sheila M. Lambert

1955-1966 Rolls-Royce Silver Cloud I, II and III

Many Rolls-Royce enthusiasts consider the Silver Cloud the most iconic of post-World War II luxury vehicles. The elegant, sweeping designs of the Silver Cloud by famed auto designer and Rolls-Royce Chief Styling Engineer John Polwhele Blatchley and by custom coachbuilders immediately convey the impression that this is a special motorcar.

Whereas the Silver Shadows and Silver Spirit series from the mid-1960s to late 1990s may sometimes get lost in the crowd, the Silver Cloud turns heads everywhere it goes.

First introduced in April 1955 and produced at the Crewe facility through March 1966, the Silver Clouds had a steel-body, with higher quality steel than used in earlier post World War II models, so there is less problem with rust. Doors, bonnet and boot top are of an aluminum alloy. The body, whether provided by Rolls-Royce from Pressed Steel Company – the majority of Silver Clouds -- or by an outside custom coachbuilder, was affixed to a rigid welded chassis frame.

The first Silver Clouds used a 155-horsepower in-line six-cylinder engine, with General Motors-sourced automatic transmission. The Silver Cloud II with V-8 engine was introduced in 1958, and the Silver Cloud III, with an improved V-8 with hardened crankshaft and more power, arrived in 1963. All Clouds had four-wheel drum brakes, with twin master cylinders from 1956. Power steering and air-conditioning were available from 1956, and power windows from 1959. The Silver Cloud III had quad headlights.

A total of 7,372 Silver Clouds were produced, including all versions. The Bentley S-Series (S1, S2 and S3) is very similar. It is essentially the same vehicle as the Cloud except with a different name badge and different radiator grill. A total of 7,475 of the Bentley S-Series were produced for a total of nearly 15,000.

The downside of buying a Silver Cloud today is the cost. Our database of Silver Clouds on the market in 2015 shows a median asking price of $73,900, with a range of $12,500 (for a vehicle not in running condition) to more than $770,000, for a rare convertible in *Concours* condition. The mean asking price is nearly $120,000. Of course, asking and actual selling price are different things, and the Price Condition Range shows Good to Excellent condition Clouds are valued at $50,000 to $100,000.

Unlike the Silver Shadow and Silver Spirit series vehicles, Silver Clouds have been enjoying strong appreciation in recent years, especially for later year versions such as the Silver Cloud III. Rare and sought-after convertibles go for several hundred thousand dollars.

Facts and Stats

Here are some key facts about the Silver Cloud series.

Engine:

Silver Cloud I: 4.9-liter (4,887 cc) in-line six-cylinder with twin carburetors providing an output of 155 hp

Silver Cloud II: 6.2-liter (6,230 cc) V-8 with aluminum block and head, gear-driven camshafts and twin carburetors delivering 200 hp

Silver Cloud III: 6.2 liter (6,230 cc) V-8 with larger carburetors and 9:1 compression delivering 216 hp

Transmission: 4-speed GM automatic

Wheelbase: 123 inches; long-wheelbase version 127 inches

Length: 212 inches; long-wheelbase version 216 inches

Weight: 4,647 lbs. (regular wheelbase)

Base price when introduced in 1955 model year: 5,078 British pounds (US$14,200 in 1955 dollars or US$125,000 in today's dollars)

Performance

Top Speed Silver Cloud I 103 mph, Silver Cloud II 114 mph, Silver Cloud III 115 mph

0-60 mph Silver Cloud I 13.5 seconds, Silver Cloud II 10.9 seconds, Silver Cloud III 10.6 seconds

Fuel Economy Silver Cloud I 12 mpg, Silver Cloud II 11 mpg, Silver Cloud III 11 mpg with most models requiring high-octane premium gas

Standard Features: Silver Cloud I with in-line 4.9-liter six-cylinder with a heritage that dated back to 1922; Silver Cloud II and III had a new mostly aluminum 6.2-liter V-8; power steering and air-conditioning optional from 1956 on short wheelbase models, standard on long wheelbase; power windows optional from 1959; four-wheel drum brakes (two master cylinders and two separate circuits) with 15-inch wheels; sealed grease points requiring lubrication only every 10,000 miles

Pros and Cons of the Silver Cloud Series
Pros:

Elegant, iconic styling certain to turn heads anywhere you go

Though in some ways not a "modern" car, the Silver Cloud, especially the later models such as the Silver Cloud III, offer a pleasurable driving experience with commanding view over the bonnet and firm but smooth and very quiet ride

Typically beautiful interior finishings, with wood veneers, Connolly leather and rich carpets

Potential for significant appreciation of vehicles, especially those in Good or better condition

Cons:

Significantly more expensive to buy now than Silver Shadow and Silver Spirit series, with a median asking price of about $74,000

Original Silver Cloud I was somewhat underpowered with its six-cylinder engine

Silver Cloud II V-8 engine crankshafts had tendency to break

Not quite a "modern" vehicle in terms of construction, ride and braking – the last major Rolls-Royce and Bentley series to have separate body and chassis, drum brakes and live rear axle

Now 50 to 60 years since last manufactured, many parts difficult to find or very expensive

Relatively limited boot (trunk) space, especially in models with the refrigeration unit in the boot

Fuel economy is poor

Other Options for the Specialist Buyer

1971-1995 Rolls-Royce Corniche

For those who prefer a two-door, the Corniche is your vehicle. First introduced in 1971 on the Silver Shadow template, the Corniche continued in production with various changes for about a quarter of a century. A total of 5,563 were produced, in addition to a much smaller number of Bentleys of the same ilk, which from 1984 were called Bentley Continentals.

The name Corniche comes from the French and Italian words for a coastal road. Designed by J. P. Blatchley, the company's chief styling engineer, the Corniche has a dashing, insouciant yet ultimately elegant air. The most desirable (and expensive) Corniche models are the drophead -- convertible -- coupés.

The median asking price for Corniches is around $48,000, although hardtops in poor condition go for as little as $15,000. The median price for convertibles is higher, around $65,000, and dropheads with low mileage and in excellent condition easily top $100,000.

1985-1997 Bentley Turbo R

For performance, consider the Bentley Turbo R. This is a car with power, style and handling (after all, the R stood for Roadholding). The early Bentley Turbo R cars inherited the turbocharged Rolls-Royce 6.75-liter V-8 from the Bentley Mulsanne Turbo, produced beginning in 1980. The turbocharged aluminum V-8 produced close to 300 horsepower, and the Turbo R's 50% stiffer suspension than the Mulsanne gave this luxury car a sportscar-style ride.

In 1987 twin carbs were replaced in the Turbo R by Bosch fuel injection, creating even more torque and better performance, and anti-lock brakes also were added. *Motor Trend* magazine called this the first Bentley in decades to truly deserve the Bentley name.

A total of 7,230 Bentley Turbo R vehicles were produced over a 12-year period at the Crewe factory. When new in the 1980s, the Turbo R sold for around $195,000 (about $450,000 in today's depreciated dollars), but the median asking price of the Turbo R now is around $25,000, with the range of $10,000 to $50,000+. Thus, a used Bentley Turbo R provides performance and handling at a reasonably affordable price.

2003-2008 Bentley

If you have the cash, want a dependable super-luxury car that you can get serviced at a dealer (though at a price), our recommendation is to look at Bentleys from around 2003 to 2008, or even newer. These are cars built at Crewe by Volkswagen.

The 21st century Bentley (and Rolls-Royce) cars experience drastic depreciation once they leave the showroom. Depending on the model, you'll find a good number of 21st century Bentley cars with asking prices from around $50,000 to $150,000. Convertibles tend to be priced higher, as do low-mileage later model vehicles. Bentley cars from this period are considerably less expensive than Rolls-Royce cars of the same age. The median asking price in our database for 2003-08 Bentleys is $69,000. For that you can get a low-mileage (often under 25,000 miles) Flying Spur or Continental.

Chassis Numbers and VIN

As noted elsewhere, until the post World War II period, Rolls-Royce generally produced just the rolling chassis – the engine, the chassis and the mechanical components from the instrument panel forward. Coachbuilders, whether independent or controlled by Rolls-Royce, produced the bodies and interiors.

The company philosophy regarding chassis numbers was that every chassis should have a unique number by which it was to be known. This concept is similar to today's VIN (Vehicle Identification Number) system. Detailed records were kept of every vehicle produced, which allowed the company to trace each individual car, or at least the sub-assemblies that went to make up the car. This was an important factor in quality control and the level of service offered by the company to its customers.

Chassis numbers were grouped into series. Beginning with the 40/50 (later called Silver Ghost) in 1907 a chassis was given a number, issued in blocks of consecutive numbers. Exactly how the blocks were chosen is unclear. In 1913, an alpha-numeric system was introduced.

Up through the Silver Cloud III, the chassis number comprised three letters (four in the case of left-hand drive vehicles), followed by a one- to three-digit number. For example, a Silver Cloud II with left-hand drive might have the chassis number LSYD324. Phantoms used a slightly different chassis numbering system. Many books on Rolls-Royce and Bentley and most enthusiasts' clubs publish list of chassis numbers by year and model of production.

The company also employed an engine number system. In general, the engine number is related to the chassis number, but there are exceptions. For one thing, traditionally the number 13 was omitted from chassis numbers but included in engine numbers, so after the 12th chassis in a series was produced, the engine number varied slightly. Again, many books and most enthusiasts' clubs publish list of engine numbers by year and model of production.

Vehicle Identification Numbers (VIN) have been in use since 1954. However, from 1954 to 1980 different manufacturers used different VIN systems, so there was no standardization.

In 1981, the United States through the U.S. National Highway Traffic Safety Administration introduced a standardized 17-place alpha-numeric Vehicle Identification Number (VIN) system, which is now in use for vehicles sold in the U.S., Canada and some other countries, although three other competing systems are also in use, in Europe, Australia and elsewhere.

Because of their large market in North America, Rolls-Royce (and Bentley) followed this VIN system, starting in October 1980 with the Silver Spirit series, and also for Corniche, Camargue and Phantom models carried over.

The VIN system effectively replaced and improved upon the chassis and engine numbering system, but being traditional and slow to change Rolls-Royce continued to use the chassis and engine numbering system as well as the VIN system. Rolls-Royce collectors' and enthusiasts' clubs still embrace the old system, alongside the VIN system for later model vehicles, and you will see front license plates sporting the vehicle's chassis number. Advertisements and editorial material in the magazines of these clubs typically use a chassis number rather than a VIN to identify even modern cars such as the 1980s and 1990s Silver Spirit and Silver Spur series. For example, the author's 1991 Silver Spur II is usually listed in club materials as NAM34693 rather than with its VIN of SCAZN02D4MCX34693.

The first 12 places in the 17-digit VIN have specific meanings designed to identify the manufacturer, chassis type, body type, engine type, fuel system, occupant restraint system, year, factory where produced, left-hand or right-hand drive, and a check number. The remaining five places in the VIN are a sequential identification number for the specific vehicle.

The following VIN positions refer to Rolls-Royce and Bentley vehicles produced primarily from 1980 to 1998:

Place position 1-3: World Manufacturer Identifier. SCA is Rolls-Royce and SCB is Bentley.

4: Chassis or Underframe Type. P is a Phantom VI, Y is Camargue and early Corniches and Z is all other models.

5: Body Type. S is saloon, L is long wheelbase with division, J is Camargue, M is Phantom VI Limousine, N is long wheelbase without division, D is convertible, T is Phantom V Landaulette, A is Phantom VI Limousine. From the 1987 model year, L and T were dropped and the following symbols were added: E is Bentley Eight, M is Phantom VI, N is long wheelbase with or without division, F is Bentley 8 L, R is Bentley Turbo R, P is Bentley Turbo

RL, X is Silver Spur and Mulsanne L Limousine, W is Silver Spur II Touring Limousine, B is Bentley Continental R and S, E is Bentley Brooklands, P is Bentley Turbo S, K is Bentley Azure and U is Bentley Continental T.

6 and 7: Type of Fuel Feed (from 1987). 00 is naturally aspirated, fuel injected, 01 is naturally aspirated, carburetors, 02 is naturally aspirated with fuel injection, 03 is turbocharged, catalyst equipped and 04 is turbocharged.

8: Occupant Restraint System: A is active seat belts, B is passive seat belts, C is air bags, D is driver-only air bag and 0 is other than America.

9: Check Digit. The check digit is 0 to 9 or X. It is used in a formula to assure that the VIN is legitimate.

10: Year: A is 1980, B is 1981, C is 1982, D is 1983, E is 1984, F is 1985, G is 1986, H is 1987, J is 1988, K is 1989, L is 1990, M is 1991, N is 1992, P is 1993, R is 1984, S is 1995, T is 1996, U is 1997, W is 1998, X is 1999 and Y is 2000. Model years 2001 to 2009 are encoded as the digits 1 to 9, and subsequent years revert to letters, encoded as A, B, C, etc.

11: Factory. C is Crewe, W is Willesden (where only the Phantom VI chassis was produced).

12: Steering Position. H is right-hand drive and X is left-hand drive.

13-17: Sequential Identification Number. These commenced with 01001 in 1980. This number is unique to each vehicle, but manufacturers use their own sequential system.

Note: In 2008, the US National Highway Traffic Safety Administration made some changes to the VIN system to assure that it could be continued in use until at least 2030.

Financing and Insuring Your Rolls-Royce or Bentley

Statistics on the subject are spotty, but anecdotal evidence suggests that most buyers of used Rolls-Royce and Bentley vehicles pay cash. If a loan is involved, it may come from a personal line of credit, home equity loan or personal loan, rather than traditional auto loan financing. However, there are lenders who have a specialty in the classic car niche, and a few banks and auto financing institutions will finance classic cars, though most regular auto lenders don't understand classic cars and don't get involved in classic car financing. You may even be able to lease your classic car, although that is rarely done.

In most cases the interest will be higher on used cars of any type than on new cars. For example, in mid-2015 the average 48-month new car loan was a little under 3%, whereas the average used car loan rate for the same financing period was almost 5%.

If you find a lender who will finance your classic Rolls-Royce or Bentley, you should expect to make a down payment of from 10 to 30% and pay an interest rate of 5% as much as 10%.

Similarly, many regular auto insurance companies, including Allstate, State Farm, GEICO, Progressive, Safeco and others provide insurance on used Rolls-Royce and Bentley vehicles, but there also are specialized insurance companies that insure classic (including antique, vintage and veteran) motorcars. In fact, because many classic car owners don't drive their cars every day, insurance costs for your classic Rolls-Royce or Bentley may well be lower than for a 2012 Camry. Keep in mind that classic car insurance is a somewhat different animal from regular auto insurance. It is advisable to have guaranteed or agreed value insurance, meaning that in the event of a total loss you will receive that amount.

Here are a few of the national and international options for vehicle financing and insurance. This is not by any means an exhaustive list. Note also that the main Rolls-Royce and Bentley owners'/enthusiasts' clubs can usually connect their members with a lender or insurance company.

Financing

Among lenders that offer classic car loans are:

J. J. Best Banc and Co.
60 N. Water Street
New Bedford, MA 02740

800-871-1965
www.jjbest.com
Reportedly the world's largest classic and collector car lender; also offers classic car insurance

Woodside Credit
19700 Fairchild Road
Irvine, CA 92612
800-717-5180
www.woodsidecredit.com

XCEL Federal Credit Union
P.O. BOX 2618
Secaucus, NJ 07096
800-284-8663
www.excelfcu.org
Has a relationship with the Rolls-Royce Owners' Club

Insurance

Footman James
Castlegate House
Castlegate Way
Dudley, West Midlands DY1 4TA, U.K.
44 (0) 333 207 6120
www.footmanjames.co.uk

Grundy Insurance
Grundy Worldwide
Division of Philadelphia Insurance Companies
866-338-4006
www.grundy.com or www.grundyworldwide.com

Hagerty Insurance
141 River's Edge Drive
Traverse City, MI 19684
877-922-9701

www.hagerty.com
Said to be the world's largest issuer of classic car insurance; publishes a magazine and an online and book-format classic car price guide and offers other services

J.C. Taylor Antique Auto Insurance Agency
320 S. 69th Street
Upper Darby, PA 19082
800-345-8290
www.jctaylor.com

Lancaster Insurance Services, Ltd.
Lancaster House
Meadow Lane
St. Ives, Cambs PE27 4ZB, U.K.
44 (0)1480 484826
www.lancasterinsurance.co.uk

R.H. Specialist Insurance
Library House
New Road
Brentwood, Essex CM14 4GD, U.K.
44 (0)1277 206911
www.rhclassicinsurance.co.uk
Has a relationship with the Rolls-Royce Enthusiasts' Club

Where to Find Your Car

There are three general ways to find used Rolls-Royce and Bentley cars: at auctions, from dealers and from individual sellers.

Auctions

The good thing about automobile auctions is that you may luck into a real bargain. That's because a significant number of sellers at auctions don't set a reserve price (the minimum price at which the vehicle can be sold), so some cars go cheaply. Overall, auction prices on all but rare collectible cars are usually 20 to 40% lower than prices from dealers or from individuals. On the negative side, you may have to travel a long distance to attend the auction, pay a fee to attend (usually there's a fee that includes both admittance to the auction and a copy of the catalog) and you rarely will have a chance to drive the vehicle(s) in which you are interested. You probably will be able to see the cars before the auction and give them a cursory inspection but you may not be able to have your mechanic give the cars a complete inspection, so unless you are already familiar with the vehicle you run the risk that while the car looks good it has hidden defects. Most auctions state that vehicles are sold "as is."

Further, most auctions require a buyer's premium, typically 10 to 15% of the final bid, so a good part of the savings you achieve by a low bid is eaten up by the buyer's premium. You also will have to be ready to pay for the vehicle immediately and be prepared to take it away, so you'll need to arrange insurance and possibly trailering quickly. Otherwise, you may incur storage fees.

Still, visiting auctions provides an education, and the results will give you more information on demand for and prices on the models you are interested in.

These are some of the better-known auction companies in the U.S., U.K. and continental Europe. Their websites provide information on upcoming classic car auctions, and many provide sales results from previous auctions.

Auctions America - www.auctionsamerica.com
Barrett-Jackson - www.barrett-jackson.com
Bonhams - www.bonhams.com/cars
British Car Auctions - www.bca-europe.com
Coys - www.coys.co.uk

H&H - www.classic-auctions.com
Hobbs Parker Car Auctions – www.hobbsparker.co.uk/cars
Mecum Auctions - www.mecum.com
RM - www.rmauctions.com
Silver - www.silverauctions.com

Online car sites such as eBay (www.ebay.com), ClassicCars.com (www.classiccars.com) and Hemmings (www.hemmings.com) do auctions.

Note that while these sites offer a variety of valuable protections for buyers, some unscrupulous sellers use dubious techniques such as multiple phony accounts to manipulate auctions. The author once won an auction at a very low price for a Rolls-Royce presented in glowing terms by a Texas used-car dealer as a low-mileage, near *Concours*-quality vehicle offered without reserve. After paying the required deposit, I was contacted by a dealer representative who claimed that an error had been made and that the vehicle was not actually as described. "This is not a car you would want," he emailed me. Obviously, someone at the dealership had slipped up and let the auction end with a winning bid below the dealer's cost. I decided this was not a dealer with whom I wanted to do business, so I demanded the return of my deposit (which I received) and notified eBay, which took no action of which I'm aware. A few weeks later, I saw the same car being advertised on eBay by the same dealer at the original price. *Caveat emptor.*

Dealers

At any given time, dealer offerings make up about three-fourths of Rolls-Royce and Bentley cars advertised on classic car sites and in enthusiast magazines.

There are two kinds of dealers to consider: Authorized Bentley or Rolls-Royce dealers have "pre-owned" cars for sale that in most cases have been traded in on a new or later model vehicle. Independent dealers specializing in classic cars advertise nationally and internationally the vehicles that they have bought from individuals or at auction or that were traded in for another car.

If you visit the major online car sales sites, especially those dealing in classic cars, such as Hemmings, Classic Cars, Vintage Driving Machines and Classic Cars for Sale, you quickly recognize the dealers who have a significant number of Rolls-Royce and Bentley cars for sale. In the U.S. these include The Auto Collections (Las Vegas), Beverly Hills Car Club (Beverly Hills), Blackhawk

Collection (Danville, Calif.), Chequered Flag International (Marina Del Rey, Calif.), Domani Motor Cars (Deerfield Beach, Fla.), Gateway Classic Cars (O'Fallon, Ill.), Gullwing Motor Cars (Astoria, N.Y.), Heritage Classics (West Hollywood, Calif.), Hyman Ltd., (St. Louis), Motorcar Gallery (Fort Lauderdale, Fla.), Park-Ward Motors (Carey, Ill.), Significant Cars (Indianapolis), Streetside Classics (Atlanta) and others. In the U.K. there are Cheshire Classic Cars (Chester), Top 555 (Oakham, Rutland) and others.

There also are a relative handful of dealers who specialize in Rolls-Royce and Bentley cars, perhaps along with a few other luxury cars such as Mercedes-Benz. Among these in the U.S. are Classic Motors (Van Nuys, Calif.), Charles S. Crail Automobiles (Santa Barbara, Calif.), Executive Motor Works (Boca Raton, Fla.), Palma Classic Cars (Audubon, N.J.). In the U.K. dealers include Frank Dale & Stepsons (London), Ghost Motors (Claygate Cross, Kent), Hanwells of London (London), P & A Wood (Dunmow, Essex), Sargeants and Goudhurst (Goudhurst, Kent), The Real Car Company (Bethesda, North Wales), Stewart Walker Ltd. (Newbury, Berkshire) and Vintage & Prestige (Grays, Essex). Typically these specialists advertise in the owners' and enthusiasts' club magazines.

Among the advantages of buying from a dealer are that you probably will have a number of vehicles from which to choose; the dealer likely will have taken care of the most significant mechanical and appearance problems that the car may have had (though you should still insist on a complete inspection by a trained mechanic); often, the hassle factor working with a dealer may be lower, since the dealer will be experienced in handling title transfers and shipping vehicles and may offer assistance in financing or insurance; in a few cases, the dealer may offer some sort of limited and probably short warranty on the car. The disadvantage of buying from a dealer is that you almost always will pay more than buying at auction or from an individual. The dealer has an overhead to cover and must mark up the price to assure a profit on the sale.

Individuals

About one-fourth of the offerings for Rolls-Royce and Bentley cars for sale that you run across are from individuals. These ads appear in the enthusiasts' and owners' club magazines, on online sales sites such as eBay Motors, Craigslist, Hemmings.com and ClassicCars.com and in local media such as daily newspapers and classified ad publications.

BUY A CLASSIC ROLLS-ROYCE OR BENTLEY

Cars sold by owners are usually priced mid-way between prices at auctions and dealers, but some owners may have an unrealistic or inflated – or simply uninformed – view of the value of their car.

Of course, you need to employ the same procedures and cautions as when buying from a dealer or at auction: See the car in person, look carefully at written service records, try to make contact with the owner directly, have the car inspected, get a CarFax or other vehicle history report and follow sensible procedures in transferring title and funds. Most owners won't willfully lie about the history and condition of the car they are trying to sell, but many do conveniently forget certain mechanical or cosmetic problems or exaggerate the condition of the vehicle.

In most cases an individual who is a member of the Rolls-Royce and Bentley clubs, such as Rolls-Royce Owners' Club, Rolls-Royce Enthusiasts' Club and Bentley Drivers Club, is the most-trusted source for a car. This is especially the case if the individual selling is a long-time, active and well-respected member of the club.

Show up in a car like this 1993 Silver Spur III Mulliner Park Ward Touring Limousine and you have ARRIVED Photo by Sheila M. Lambert

Selling Your Car

Should frustration, health, expense, the desire to buy a different car or just the need to raise cash cause you to decide to sell your beloved Rolls-Royce or Bentley, you basically have the same options for selling it as you did when buying it – place an individual for-sale ad, sell to a dealer or sell at auction. Reread the above chapter for more information and on the pros and cons of each option. In general, you'll get more for your car through an individual sale, less from a dealer and perhaps much less at auction, especially if you sell it without reserve.

In addition to the car dealers and auction companies listed in the chapter above, a handful of companies and individuals actively seek to buy used Rolls-Royce and Bentley cars, either as part of a collection or singly. A majority buy outright, but some take your car on assignment. Most advertise in the owners' and enthusiasts' club magazines.

Remember, unless you sell individual-to-individual or take your chances at auction, you'll be selling at wholesale. Except for a true collector's item, or rare vehicles that are appreciating in value, you'll likely to have to sell for less than you paid, even before factoring in the repair and maintenance costs you've incurred. The fact that you have put thousands or tens of thousands of dollars into your car in repair and restoration costs does not necessarily mean it is worth much more than any other car of its age, model and condition. Having your car in top condition makes it more pleasurable to own, and likely will make it easier to sell, but that does not assure that you will regain the money you invested in it or make a profit on it.

A final option for the near-desperate is to sell the car for parts. Several companies, including Luxury Junkyard near Greenville, S.C., buy and dismantle cars for parts. Other companies also buy cars for parts. Let's hope a parts graveyard isn't the final resting place of your vehicle.

Rolls-Royce and Bentley Enthusiast Clubs

If you are considering buying a Rolls-Royce or Bentley, it's well worth your time and money to join one or more of the owners' and enthusiasts' clubs. Most of these clubs are open not just to Rolls-Royce and Bentley owners but to anyone interested in these motorcars.

By joining and participating in one or more of these clubs you benefit in several different ways. First, there's the social aspect. You'll get to hob-knob with a diverse bunch of people who, though they come from many different backgrounds, share a common interest in Rolls-Royce or Bentley motorcars. Just as important is what you can learn about buying and maintaining a vehicle. Most of these clubs have newsletters or magazines filled with news and informative technical articles. The ads in these publications will introduce you to many resources for finding parts, restoring vintage vehicles and buying and selling cars. Most clubs also have an online forum or bulletin board where as a member you can ask questions and get answers from many experts. Finally, these clubs are great sources for helping you find a well-cared for vehicle at a competitive price. Here are some of the leading owners' clubs:

Rolls-Royce Owners' Club (RROC), 191 Hempt Road, Mechanicsburg, PA 17050, phone 717-697-4671, www.rroc.org, email rrochq@rroc.org

Founded in 1951 by six enthusiasts with a membership of around 200 in its first year, the Rolls-Royce Owners' Club now has more than 7,500 members primarily in the United States but also in about 50 other countries. It welcomes both Rolls-Royce and Bentley owners – RROC members have around 5,000 Rolls-Royces and 2,000 Bentleys. It also welcomes those who don't who simply have an interest in these cars.

The club has its national headquarters in Mechanicsburg, Penn., near the state capital of Harrisburg. The current executive director of the RROC is Bob Austin. The RROC publishes a professionally designed and edited magazine, *The Flying Lady*, six times a year. This magazine includes a classified section with listings of vehicles, parts and services for sale. The club also publishes an annual membership directory, with contact information on members, including the car or cars that they own. This is an invaluable tool in locating other Rolls and Bentley enthusiasts in your area or when you travel.

Two classics displayed at a Southeast Regional Rolls-Royce Owners' Club meet near Greenville, S.C., in 2014 – a 1934 Rolls-Royce 20/25 (left) owned by Richard and Lynn Coombs and a 1950 Bentley Mark VI (right) owned by Jeff Trepel Photo by Sheila M. Lambert

Associated with Rolls-Royce Owners' Club is the **Rolls-Royce Foundation** (www.rollsroycefoundation.org), an independent, non-profit, charitable organization dedicated to the preservation and promotion of the heritage of Rolls-Royce and Bentley motorcars. The Foundation's museum, located in the same 16,000 sq. ft. building in Mechanicsburg as the RROC, has more than 20 Rolls-Royce and Bentley cars and usually has 14 to 18 on display, ranging from a 1929 Rolls-Royce Springfield Phantom I and a 1936 Bentley $3\frac{1}{2}$-Liter to vehicles from the 1980s. A library has books, technical manuals, handbooks, sales literature and periodicals, as well as historic documents about individual vehicles. If you are looking to buy a specific vehicle, you may be able to order, for a modest charge, the "build sheet" for the car, along with initial warranty service information and perhaps other historical information. The library is available to researchers and browsers, but the materials do not circulate.

BUY A CLASSIC ROLLS-ROYCE OR BENTLEY

The RROC holds a national meeting each year in the United States. This meet, billed as the largest gathering of Rolls-Royce and Bentley enthusiasts in North America, usually runs for six days. The 2015 national meeting was in Orlando in March, and the 2016 meeting is set for late July in Asheville, N.C.

National members may also join one of 28 regional clubs around the U.S. and Canada. Most of these regional clubs have their own newsletters and hold several regional meets a year. The RROC usually also has an international event each year. These meetings are a valuable opportunity to see a lot of Rolls-Royce and Bentley models of many different periods and to learn more about their rewards and challenges of ownership from the owners themselves.

Biltmore House in Asheville, site of the 2016 national RROC meet, where members' cars will be displayed on the lawn of America's largest private home   Photo Courtesy of Biltmore Estate

In addition, the RROC has several special interest member sections for owners of different models, such as Silver Clouds and early Phantoms. There is a small fee to join these special interest groups, and several, such as The Modern Car Society for those who own or have an interest in Rolls-Royce and Bentley cars from 1965 onward, publish a newsletter or magazine.

The club' excellent website (www.rroc.org) has a discussion forum about Bentley and Rolls-Royce vehicles that is the largest online forum of its type. There is also an online store, a technical library, a technical tips section and guides to buying a used Rolls or Bentley.

Spectators and judges gather round a spectacular 1962 Silver Cloud II H. J. Mulliner drophead coupé at the 2015 national Rolls-Royce Owners' Club national meet in Orlando – note the license tag, as the owner seems to be making a tongue-in-cheek (?) statement about the cost of this Concours-*level Cloud*   Photo by Sheila M. Lambert

Dues: Primary members of the Rolls-Royce Owners' Club have the right to vote in RROC elections and other matters and receive an annual subscription to *The Flying Lady* magazine plus the annual membership directory and full access to the RROC website. As of 2015, primary members living in the United States pay annual dues of US$70.

Those living in Canada pay US$90. Members living in other countries pay US$120. In addition, there is a one-time initiation fee for all primary members of US$30. All primary members living in North America also receive free membership in one of the 28 regional sections, many of which publish their own newsletters or magazines. For those living outside North America who agree to receive all member information in digital form, there is an international digital membership with dues of US$30 a year and no initiation fee.

The spouse or partner of a primary member pays US$10 a year, but only the primary member receives *The Flying Lady* magazine and the annual directory. Spouse/partner members do have the right to vote. Junior members under age 18 pay dues of US$15 a year and receive *The Flying Lady* but do not have the right to vote.

Life memberships to RROC are available to those who have been an RROC primary member for at least 10 years. The one-time life membership fee is 20 times the normal annual dues.

Rolls-Royce Foundation membership, separate from RROC membership, costs US$30 a year or US$450 for a lifetime membership.

Rolls-Royce Enthusiasts' Club (RREC), The Hunt House, High Street, Paulerspury, Northamptonshire NN12 7NA, England, U.K., phone 44 (0)1327 811788, www.rrec.org.uk, email admin@rrec.org.uk

The Rolls-Royce Enthusiasts Club is the world's largest organization for owners and enthusiasts of Rolls-Royce motorcars of all periods and Bentleys manufactured since 1933.

Founded at Oxford in 1957 with just 11 enthusiasts, it now has a membership of around 10,000 in the U.K. and around the world.

The RREC annually produces the Annual Rally and *Concours d'Elegance*, which is said to be the largest Rolls-Royce and Bentley gathering in the world, typically with hundreds of vintage motorcars. It is held at different locations in the U.K.

RREC members received the club's 68-page magazine, *Bulletin*, six times a year, and *Advertiser*, a monthly publication that advertises Rolls-Royce and Bentley cars and services for sale.

The club has 18 sections in the U.K, many with their own meetings, shows and publications. It also has 21 overseas sections, including 17 in Europe, two in Canada, one in Japan and one in South Africa; however, it currently does not have a section in the U.S.

As with the RROC, the RREC maintains a large research library and offers historical information on individual vehicles.

Dues as of 2015 for RREC are 77 British pounds per year, plus a one-time 30-pound joining fee. Spouses/partners pay 10 pounds per year, and junior members under age 20 pay 20 pounds. Those joining after July 1 pay a discounted one-half rate for the remaining part of the year. Members outside of the U.K. who want to receive publications and information via airmail (recommended) pay an extra 27 pounds. At current exchange rates, a primary member and spouse in the U.S., with airmail delivery of materials, would pay around US$225 to join the RREC.

Bentley Drivers Club, Ltd. (BDC) W.O. Bentley Memorial Building, Ironstone Lane, Wroxton, Banbury, Oxfordshire OX15 6ED, England, U.K., phone 44 (0)1295 738886, www.bdcl.org, email memberships@bdcl.org

Founded in London in 1936 by Keston Pelmore, a young Bentley owner, the Bentley Drivers Club has grown to its present membership of about 3,700. Although it is based in England and much of its membership is in the U.K., it has members in most countries of the world.

The club's nine geographical regions are the U.K., Australia, New Zealand, Germany, Switzerland, The Netherlands, Japan, South Africa and the United States.

The BDC is open to Bentley enthusiasts whether or not they own a Bentley. However, only those who currently own a Bentley, or who have owned one in the past, can become full members.

Those who have never owned a Bentley can join as associate members.

The club puts out three main publications: the bi-monthly *BDC Review* magazine with articles by BDC members, the monthly *Diary* with information on club events and the bi-monthly *Advertiser* with ads for cars, parts and services.

The BDC also has a discussion forum on its website, an online store, a spare parts program, an auto insurance program (for the U.K.) and a members directory.

The club's key member events in the U.K. include an Annual Summer Rally and *Concours d'Elegance* in June, an Annual Sprint meeting in Warwickshire and an Annual Race Meeting at Silverstone in August. There are also numerous local events in the U.K. and occasional international events.

Dues: As of 2015, fees for full members and associate members are 102 British pounds in the U.K. and 95 pounds outside the U.K., plus in both cases a one-time set-up fee of 50 pounds. Thus, members outside the U.K. would pay about US$225 to join the club, at current exchange rates.

Family members are an additional 15 pounds each, and there are reduced fees for young people.

Other Clubs

Classic Car Club of America (CCCA), P.O. Box 346160, Chicago, IL 60634, 847-390-0443, www.classiccarclub.org, email headquartersinfo@classiccarclub.org

The Classic Car Club of America focuses on what it calls cars from the "Grand Classic Era" of 1919-1948. So-called "full classic" cars of this period include Rolls-Royce and Bentley, along with Cadillac, Packard, Lincoln, Alfa Romeo, Nash and others.

The club operates a museum in Hickory Corners, Mich., publishes a magazine and presents national and regional events. Annual membership fee for U.S. residents is US$70.

Rolls-Royce Owners' Club of Australia, www.rroc.org.au

Rolls-Royce & Bentley Club of New Zealand, www.nzrrbc.co.nz

Rolls-Royce and Bentley Dealerships

Here are lists of Rolls-Royce and Bentley dealerships in the U.S., Canada and the U.K.

ROLLS-ROYCE

Rolls-Royce dealerships in Canada are listed alphabetically by city name; in the United Kingdom alphabetically by country and then by city; in the United States alphabetically by state and then by city within the state. Currently, Rolls-Royce has four authorized dealerships in Canada, six in the U.K. and 36 in the U.S.

For dealerships in other countries, visit the main Rolls-Royce website at www.rolls-roycemotorcars.com.

Keep in mind that most of these dealerships are focused on sales and service of Rolls-Royce motorcars from 2003 onward, when BMW took over the Rolls-Royce name and trademarks.

Some Rolls-Royce dealers are also dealers for Bentley and other upper-end vehicles.

Note: When dialing from abroad, the telephone country code must be dialed first. The country code for the U.S. and Canada is 1 and the country code for the U.K. is 44. The U.S. and Canada have three-digit area codes and the U.K. has area codes of two, three, four or five digits, all starting with a 0. The telephone numbers below do not include the 1 for the U.S. and Canada but do include 44 for the U.K.

CANADA

Rolls-Royce Motor Cars Alberta
204 Meridian Road NE
Alberta, Alberta T2A 2NR
403-273-6060
www.rolls-roycemotorcars-alberta.com/

Rolls-Royce Motor Cars Quebec

BUY A CLASSIC ROLLS-ROYCE OR BENTLEY

5155 Rue de Sorel
Montreal, Quebec H4P 1G7
514-738-3030
www.rolls-roycemotorcars-quebec.com/

Rolls-Royce Motor Cars Toronto
740 Dupont Street
Toronto, Ontario M6G 1Z6
416-530-1880
www.rolls-roycemotorcars-toronto.com/

Rolls-Royce Motor Cars Vancouver
1727 West 5th Avenue
Vancouver, British Columbia V6J 3H5
604-659-3208
www.rolls-roycemotorcars-vancouver.com/

UNITED KINGDOM

Rybrook, Authorised Rolls-Royce Motor Cars Dealer
2635 Stratford Road
Hockley Heath, Solihull
Birmingham, West Midlands, England B94 5NH
44 (0)1564 787170
www.rolls-roycemotorcars-birmingham.co.uk/

Rolls-Royce Motor Cars Edinburgh
Bankhead Drive
Sighthill Industrial Estate
Edinburgh, Scotland EH11 4DJ
44 (0)131 442 1000
www.rolls-roycemotorcars-edinburgh.co.uk/

Rolls-Royce Motor Cars London
15 Berkeley Square
London, England W1J 6EG
44 (0)333 240 7220

www.rolls-roycemotorcars-london.co.uk/

P&A Wood, Authorised Rolls-Royce Motor Cars Dealer
Great Easton, Dunmow
Essex, England CM6 2HD
44 (0)1371 852000
www.rolls-roycemotorcars-pawood.co.uk/

Rolls-Royce Motor Cars Manchester
Manchester Road
Knutsford, Cheshire WA16 0ST
44 (0)1565 700 000
www.rolls-roycemotorcars-manchester.co.uk/

Rolls-Royce Motor Cars Sunningdale
London Road
Sunningdale, Berkshire SL5 0EX
44 (0)1344 871200
www.rolls-roycemotorcars-sunningdale.co.uk/

UNITED STATES
Arizona
Rolls-Royce Motor Cars Scottsdale
7111 East Chauncy Lane
Phoenix, AZ 85054
480-538-4300
www.rolls-roycemotorcars-scottsdale.com/

California
Rolls-Royce Motor Cars Beverly Hills
8845 West Olympic Blvd.
Beverly Hills, CA
310-659-4050
www.rolls-roycemotorcars-beverlyhills.com/

Rolls-Royce Motor Cars Los Gatos

BUY A CLASSIC ROLLS-ROYCE OR BENTLEY

620 Blossom Hill Road
Los Gatos, CA 95039
408-354-4000
www.rolls-roycemotorcars-losgatos.com/

Rolls-Royce Motor Cars San Diego
7440 La Jolla Blvd
La Jolla, CA 92037
858-454-1800
www.rolls-roycemotorcars-lajolla.com/

Rolls-Royce Motors Cars Orange County
4040 Campus Drive
Newport Beach, CA 92660
949-333-8100
www.rolls-roycemotorcars-oc.com/

Rolls-Royce Motor Cars Pasadena
337 West Colorado Blvd
Pasadena, CA 91105
626-449-0770
www.rolls-roycemotorcars-pasadena.com/

Rolls-Royce Motor Cars Rancho Mirage
71-387 Highway 111
Rancho Mirage, CA 92270
760-773-5000
www.rolls-roycemotorcars-pasadena.com/

Rolls-Royce Motor Cars Westlake
3610 East Thousand Oaks Blvd
Thousand Oaks, CA 91362
805-418-9092
www.rolls-roycemotorcars-westlake.com

Connecticut
Rolls-Royce Motor Cars Greenwich
275 West Putnam Avenue
Greenwich, CT 06830
203-661-4430
www.rolls-roycemotorcars-greenwich.com/

Florida
Rolls-Royce Motor Cars Lauderdale
200 East Sunrise Boulevard
Fort Lauderdale, FL 33304
954-779-2009
www.rolls-roycemotorcars-fortlauderdale.com/

Rolls-Royce Motor Cars Orlando/Fields Motorcars Orlando
895 North Ronald Regan Boulevard
Longwood, FL 32750
407-339-3443
www.rolls-roycemotorcars-orlando.com/ or www.fieldsmotorcarsorlando.com

Rolls-Royce Motor Cars Miami
2060 Biscayne Boulevard
Miami, FL 33137
305-571-1205
www.rolls-roycemotorcars-miami.com/

Rolls-Royce Motor Cars Naples
900 Tamiami Trail North
Naples, FL 34102
239-263-6070
www.rolls-roycemotorcars-naples.com/

Rolls-Royce Motor Cars Tampa Bay
3333 Gandy Boulevard
Pinellas Park, FL 33781
727-822-2019

www.rolls-roycemotorcars-tampa.com/

Rolls-Royce Motor Cars Palm Beach
2901 Okeechobee Blvd
West Palm Beach, FL 33409
561-684-6666
www.rolls-roycemotorcars-palmbeach.com/

Georgia
Rolls-Royce Motor Cars Atlanta
3040 Piedmont Road
Atlanta, GA 30305
404-237-6200
www.rolls-roycemotorcars-georgia.com/

Illinois
Rolls-Royce Motor Cars Gold Coast
834 North Rush Street
Chicago, IL 60611
312-280-4848
www.rolls-roycemotorcars.goldcoast.com/

Steve Foley, Inc., Authorised Rolls-Royce Motor Cars Dealer
100 N. Skokie Boulevard
Northbrook, IL 60062
847-564-4090
www.rrmc-stevefoley.com/

Massachusetts
Herb Chambers Rolls-Royce Motor Cars New England
533 Boston Post Road
Wayland, MA 01778
508-401-2700
www.rolls-roycemotorcars-newengland.com/

Michigan
Rolls-Royce Motor Cars Michigan
1755 C Maplelawn Drive
Troy, MI 48084
866-534-2087
www.rolls-roycemotorcars-michigan.com/

Missouri
Rolls-Royce Motor Cars St Louis
9 Arnage Drive
Chesterfield, St Louis, MO 63005
Phone: 636-449-0000
www.rolls-roycemotorcars-stlouis.com/

Nevada
Rolls-Royce Motor Cars Las Vegas
5550 West Sahara Avenue
Las Vegas, NV 89146
702-932-7100
www.rolls-roycemotorcars-lasvegas.com/

New Jersey
F.C. Kerbeck & Sons, Authorised Rolls-Royce Motor Cars Dealer
100 Route 73 North
Palmyra, NJ 08065
856-829-8200
www.rolls-roycemotorcars-fckerbeck.com/

Paul Miller, Authorised Rolls-Royce Motor Cars Dealer
250 Route 46 West
Parsippany, NJ 07054
973-575-7751

BUY A CLASSIC ROLLS-ROYCE OR BENTLEY

www.rolls-roycemotorcars-parsippany.com/

New York
Rolls-Royce Motor Cars Long Island
115 South Service Road
Jericho, NY 11753
516-203-3030
www.rolls-roycemotorcars-longisland.com/

Rolls-Royce Motor Cars Manhattan
270 Eleventh Avenue
New York, NY 10001
212-594-6200
www.rolls-roycemotorcars-manhattan.com/

North Carolina
Rolls-Royce Motor Cars Raleigh
5601 Capital Boulevard
Raleigh, NC 27616
919-876-5432
www.rolls-roycemotorcars-raleigh.com/

Ohio
Midwestern Auto Group, Authorised Rolls-Royce Motor Cars Dealer
6335 Perimeter Loop Road
Dublin, OH 43017
614-717-4840
www.rolls-roycemotorcars-ohio.com/

Rolls-Royce Motor Cars Cleveland
28300 Loraine Road
North Olmstead, OH 44070
440-716-2000

www.rolls-roycemotorcars-cleveland.com/

South Carolina
Rolls-Royce Motor Cars Charleston
1511 Savannah Highway
Charleston, SC 29407
www.rolls-roycemotorcars-charleston.com/

Tennessee
Rolls-Royce Motor Cars Nashville
225 Comtide Court
Franklin, TN 37067
615-261-0083
www.rolls-roycemotorcars-nashville.com/

Texas
Rolls-Royce Motor Cars Austin
12989 Research Boulevard Building B100
Austin, TX 78750
512-401-2663
www.rolls-roycemotorcars-austin.com/

Rolls-Royce Motor Cars Dallas
5300 Lemmon Avenue
Dallas, TX 75209
214-443-8240
www.rolls-roycemotorcars-dallas.com/

Rolls-Royce Motor Cars Houston
1530 West Loop South
Houston, TX 77027
713-850-1530
www.rolls-roycemotorcars-houston.com/

Virginia
Rolls-Royce Motor Cars Sterling
21826 Pacific Boulevard
Sterling, VA 20166
571-434-1944
www.rolls-roycemotorcars-sterling.com/

Washington
Rolls-Royce Motor Cars Bellevue
1882 136th Place NE, Suite 107
Bellevue, WA 98005
425-646-3111
www.rolls-roycemotorcars-bellevue.com/

BENTLEY

Bentley dealerships in Canada are listed alphabetically by city name; in the United Kingdom alphabetically by country and then by city; in the United States alphabetically by state and then by city within the state. Currently, Bentley has four authorized dealerships in Canada, 19 in the U.K. and 43 in the U.S.

For dealerships in other countries, visit the main Bentley website at www.bentleymotors.com.

A very few Bentley dealerships offer service and used car sales only and do not sell new Bentley cars. As with Rolls-Royce, most Bentley dealers make most of their money on service, not on sales.

Some Bentley dealers also sell Rolls-Royce and other upper-end vehicles, though they may be offered in different showrooms. Many dealerships have multiple websites, often including their own website and one connected to the official Bentley site.

CANADA

Bentley Calgary
150 Glendeer Circle SE

Calgary, Alberta T2H 2V4
403-208-6262
www.calgary.bentleymotors.com

Bentley Montreal
8255 Bougainville Street
Montreal, Quebec H4P 2T3
514-334-9910
www.montreal.bentleymotors.com

Bentley Toronto
740 Dupont Street
Toronto, Ontario M6G 1Z6
416-530-1880
www.toronto.bentleymotors.com

Bentley Vancouver
1730 Burrard Street
Vancouver, British Columbia V6J 3G7
604-738-5577
www.vancouver.bentleymotors.com

UNITED KINGDOM
Bentley Berkshire/H. R. Owen
Station Road
Pangbourne, Berkshire RG8 7AN
England, U.K.
44 (0)333 240 8483
www.berkshire.bentleymotors.com

Bentley Birmingham/Sytneer
2 Wingfoot Way
Fort Parkway
Birmingham B24 9HF
England, U.K.

BUY A CLASSIC ROLLS-ROYCE OR BENTLEY

44 (0)121 4488016
www.sytner.co.uk

Bentley Cambridge
383 Milton Road
Cambridge, CB4 1SR
England, U.K.
44 (0)1223 640 632
www.vindis.bentleymotors.com

Bentley Cheltenham/H. R. Owen
Rutherford Way
Cheltenham, Gloucestershire GL51 9TU
England, U.K.
44 (0)333 240 8485
www.hrowen.co.uk

Bentley Essex
Auto Way
Ipswich Road
Colchester, Essex CO4 9HA
England, U.K.
44 (0)1206 848500
www.essex.bentleymotors.com

Harwoods Bentley Hampshire
Lyndhurst
Bramshaw
Hampshire SO43 7JF
England, U.K.
44 (0)23 8001 8978
www.harwoods.uk.com/bentley/

Bentley Hertfordshire
202 - 204 High Street
Barnet, Herts EN5 5TA
England, U.K.

44 (0)20 3763 7557
www.hertfordshire.bentleymotors.com

Bentley JCT 600 Leedis Court
102 Gelderd Road
Leeds LS12 6BY
England, U.K.
44 (0)1132 440600
www.jct600.bentleymotors.com

Bentley Kent/Jardine Motors Group
92 London Road
Sevenoaks
Kent TN13 1BA
England, U.K.
44 (0)1732 314136
www.jardinemotors.co.uk/bentley

Bentley Leicester
Watermead Business Park, Syston
Leicester, Leicestershire LE7 1PF
England, U.K. United Kingdom
44 (0)116 367 8847
www.leicester.bentleymotors.com

Jack Barclay London
18 Berkeley Square
Mayfair, London W1J 6AE
England, U.K.
44 (0)20 7907 8708
www.jackbarclay.bentleymotors.com
Jack Barclay was founded in 1927; a part of the H.R. Owen Group, it is said to be the oldest and largest Bentley dealer in the world

Bentley Manchester
Mobberley Road
Knutsford WA16 8GT

BUY A CLASSIC ROLLS-ROYCE OR BENTLEY

England, U.K.
44 (0)1565 632222
www.manchester.bentleymotors.com

Bentley Newcastle
Silverlink Wallsend
Newcastle-upon-tyne, England NE28 9ND
44 (0)8443 711454
www.newcastle.bentleymotors.com

Bentley Surrey/H. R. Owen
122 Oyster Lane
Byfleet
Weybridge, Surrey KT14 7JU
England, U.K.
44 (0)1932 506807
www.surrey.bentleymotors.com

Harwoods of Sussex
London Road
Pulborough, West Sussex RH20 1AR
England, U.K.
44 (0)1798 877213
www.sussex.bentleymotors.com

Charles Hurst Ltd.
62 Boucher Road
Balmoral
Belfast BT12 6LR
Ireland, U.K.
44 (0)2890 385755
www.charleshurst.bentleymotors.com

Bentley Edinburgh
8 Whitehill Road
Fort Kinnaird
Edinburgh EH15 3HR

Scotland, U.K.
44 (0)1314 752100
www.edinburgh.bentleymotors.com

Bentley Glasgow
14 Bothwell Road
Hamilton ML3 0AY
Scotland, U.K.
44 (0)1698 303850
www.glasgow.bentleymotors.com

Bentley Cardiff
293 Penarth Road
Cardiff CF11 8TT
Wales, U.K.
44 (0)2920 347950
www.cardiff.bentleymotors.com

UNITED STATES

Arizona
Bentley Scottsdale
7171 East Chauncey Lane
Phoenix, AZ 85054
480-538-4300
www.scottsdalebentley.com

California
Bentley Beverly Hills / Ogara Coach Company
8833 West Olympic Blvd.
Beverly Hills, CA, 90211
888-294-1133
www.beverlyhills.bentleymotors.com or www.ogaracoach.com

BUY A CLASSIC ROLLS-ROYCE OR BENTLEY

Bentley Los Gatos
620 Blossom Hill Road
Los Gatos, CA 95032
408-358-7777
www.losgatos.bentleymotors.com

Bentley Newport Beach
445 East Coast Highway
Newport Beach, CA 92660
949-673-0900
www.newportbeach.bentleymotors.com

Bentley Pasadena/Rusnak
285 West Colorado Blvd.
Pasadena, CA 91105
844-242-3474
www.bentley.rusnakonline.com

Bentley Rancho Mirage
71-387 Highway 111
Rancho Mirage, CA 92270
760-773-5000
www.ranchomirage.bentleymotors.com

Bentley San Diego
11455 Sorrento Valley Road
San Diego, CA 92121
858-350-1393
www.sandiego.bentleymotors.com

Bentley San Francisco
999 Van Ness Avenue
San Francisco, CA 94019
415-351-5102
www.sanfrancisco.bentleymotors.com

Bentley Westlake
3610 East Thousand Oaks Boulevard
Thousand Oaks, CA 91362
805-418-9092
www.westlake.bentleymotors.com

Bentley Walnut Creek
1425 Parkside Drive
Walnut Creek, CA 94596
925-444-2000
www.walnutcreek.bentleymotors.com

Colorado
Bentley Denver
1480 East County Line Road
Highlands Ranch, CO 80126
303-730-7340
www.denver.bentleymotors.com

Connecticut
Bentley Greenwich
275 West Putnam Avenue
Greenwich, CT 06830
203-661-3100
www.greenwich.bentleymotors.com

Florida
Bentley Fort Lauderdale
200 East Sunrise Boulevard
Fort Lauderdale, FL 33304
954-779-2009
www.bentleyfortlauderdale.com

BUY A CLASSIC ROLLS-ROYCE OR BENTLEY

Braman Bentley Miami
2020 Biscayne Boulevard
Miami, FL 33137
305-571-1200
www.bramanbentley.net

Bentley Orlando/Fields Motorcars Orlando
895 North Ronald Reagan Boulevard
Longwood, FL 32750
407-339-3443
www.orlando.bentleymotors.com

Bentley Palm Beach
2901 Okeechobee Boulevard
West Palm Beach, FL 33409
888-920-4041
www.palmbeach.bentleymotors.com

Georgia
Bentley Atlanta
10995 Westside Parkway
678-534-7469
www.bentleyatlanta.com

Illinois
Bentley Motors Inc.
20 Currency Drive
Bloomington, IL 61704
309-829-9999
www.bentleymotorsonline.com

Bentley Gold Coast
834 North Rush Street
Chicago, IL 60611
312-280-4848

www.bentleygoldcoast.com

Bentley Downers Grove
330 Ogden Avenue
Downers Grove, IL 60515
630-241-4848
www.bentleydownersgrove.com

Bentley Northbrook
100 Skokie Boulevard
Northbrook, IL 60062
888-997-1810
www.bentleynorthbrook.com

Indiana
Bentley Zionsville/Albers
360 South First Street
Zionsville, IN, 46077
317-873 2360
www.zionsville.bentleymotors.com

Massachusetts
Bentley Boston - A Herb Chambers Company
533 Boston Post Road
Wayland, MA 01778
508-650-0020
www.bentleyboston.com

Michigan
Bentley Troy
1755-B Maplelawn Drive
Troy, MI 48084
248-519-9617
www.troy.bentleymotors.com

BUY A CLASSIC ROLLS-ROYCE OR BENTLEY

Minnesota
Bentley Minneapolis
13708 Wayzata Boulevard
Minnetonka, MN 55305
952-797-1777
www.minneapolis.bentleymotors.com

Missouri
Bentley St. Louis
One Arnage Blvd Chesterfield
St Louis, MO 63005
636-449-0000
www.stlouis.bentleymotors.com

Nevada
Bentley Las Vegas/Towbin Motors
5550 West Sahara Avenue
Las Vegas, NV 89146
702-932-7100
www.lasvegas.bentleymotors.com

New Jersey
Bentley Edison
808 US Route 1
Edison, NJ 08817
855-325-1140
www.edisonbentley.com

Bentley Palmyra/F. C. Kerbeck
100 Route 73 North
Palmyra, NJ 08065
866-416-2949

www.fckerback.com

Paul Miller Bentley Parsippany
250 U.S. 46
Parsippany, NJ 07054
973-575-7755
www.paulmillerbentley.com

New York
Bentley Long Island
115 South Service Road
Jericho, NY 11753
516-367-9600
www.longisland.bentleymotors.com

Manhattan Motorcars
270 11th Avenue
New York, NY 10001
212-594-6200
www.manhattanmotorcars.com

North Carolina
Bentley High Point
1730 North Main Street
High Point, NC 27262
336-884-1100
www.bentleyhighpoint.com

Ohio
Bentley Columbus
6335 Perimeter Loop Road
Dublin, OH 43017
614-889-2571
www.columbus.bentleymotors.com

Pennsylvania
Bentley Pittsburgh
1701 West Liberty Avenue
Pittsburgh, PA 15226
412-344-6010
www.bentleypittsburgh.com

Rhode Island
Bentley Providence
1515 Bald Hill Road
Warwick, RI 02886
401-304-3490
www.providence.bentleymotors.com

Tennessee
Music City Motor Cars
225 Comtide Court
Franklin, TN 37067
888-545-1585
www.musiccitymotorcars.com

Texas
Bentley of Austin
12989 Research Boulevard
Austin, TX 78750
512-236-8539
www.bentleyofaustin.com

Park Place Bentley Dallas
5300 Lemmon Avenue
Dallas, TX 75209
214-443-5250

www.bentleydallas.parkplace.com

Bentley Houston
1530 West Loop South
Houston, TX 77027
713-850-1530
www.bentleyhouston.com

Virginia
Bentley Tysons
8550 Leesburg Pike
Vienna, VA 22182
703-712-8324
www.tysons.bentleymotors.com

Washington
Bentley Bellevue
1808 136th Avenue NE
Bellevue, WA 98005
425-646-3111
www.bellevue.bentleymotors.com

Sources of Parts, Restoration, Repairs and Other Information

This section offers some options on obtaining Rolls-Royce and Bentley parts, on restoring and repairing these motor cars, on sources of information about these cars and on transport of vehicles by motor carrier. Sections of this chapter are devoted to the above matters, separated into geographical regions, namely the United Kingdom and Europe, the United States and Canada. This is in no way an exhaustive listing, and the usual cautions apply: Do your own due diligence before using any company listed here.

As noted elsewhere, authorized Bentley dealers usually provide service and parts not only for Bentley but also for Crewe-built Rolls-Royce cars. Many Rolls-Royce dealers provide parts and service only for vehicles from the 2003 model year onward, when BMW took obtained the Rolls-Royce brand name and trademarks. A list of authorized Rolls-Royce and Bentley dealers appears elsewhere in this book.

In many cases, your best resource for information of any type about Rolls-Royce and Bentley cars comes from the members of owners' and enthusiasts' clubs, notably the Rolls-Royce Owners' Club, the Bentley Drivers Club and the Rolls-Royce Enthusiasts' Club. Detailed information about these organizations is presented in another chapter of this book.

Parts

UNITED KINGDOM AND EUROPE
Brabo
Arnoudstraat 17
2182 DZ Hillegon – Holland
0031 252 527875
www.braboparts.com
100,000+ parts in stock

Crewe Genuine Parts
www.bentleymotors.com
Stocks 55,000 parts for Bentley and Crewe-built Rolls-Royce (1955-2002) models -- sold through authorized Bentley dealers in the U.S., U.K., Europe and elsewhere

Flying Spares Parts
Rossendale House
Station Road Industrial Estate
Market Bosworth, Warks CV13 0PE, U.K.
44 (0)1455 292949
www.flyingspares.com
New, reconditioned and recycled parts, shipped worldwide

IntroCar Ltd.
Units C&D The Pavilions, 2 East Road
Wimbledon, London, SW19 1UW, U.K.
44 (0)20 8546 2027
www.introcar.co.uk
Offers more than 300,000 parts for Rolls-Royce and Bentley cars from 1946 on, ships worldwide

T&G Auto Spares Ltd.
17 Hare Farm Avenue
Farmley, Leeds LS12 5QB, U.K.
44 (0)113 255 9908
www.tgautospares.co.uk

CANADA
Hyphen Repairs
59999 6th Line—RR3
Orton, Ontario L0N 1N0
905-670-3656

UNITED STATES
Competition Motors

BUY A CLASSIC ROLLS-ROYCE OR BENTLEY

40 Longmeadow Road
Portsmouth, NH 03801
603-431-0035
www.competitionmotorsltd.com
Specializes in pre-World War II Rolls-Royce and Bentley tools

Crewe Genuine Parts
www.bentleymotors.com
Stocks 55,000 parts for Bentley and Crewe-built Rolls-Royce (1955-2002) models -sold through authorized Bentley dealers in the U.S., U.K., Europe and elsewhere

The Luxury Junkyard
2541 N. Pleasantburg Drive, Suite S – PMB 118
Greenville, SC 29609
864-356-3343
www.theluxuryjunkyard.com
This junkyard specializes in used Rolls-Royce and Bentley parts, having parted out more than 260 vehicles; many owners, dealers and mechanics depend on this unique junkyard for hard-to-get parts

Prestigious Euro Cars
1420 N.W. 23 Ave.
Fort Lauderdale, FL 33311
954-779-1000
www.prestigiouseurocars.com
Sells new, used and re-conditioned parts; also offers repair and restoration service

Replacement Parts, Inc.
770-459-0040
www.replacementpartsinc.com
Has around 5,000 used, OEM and overhauled parts for pre-war to 21st century Rolls-Royce and Bentley cars

Jeff Trapel
704-866-4636, email jtrepel1@gmail.com
Handbooks, manuals, sales literature and books on Rolls-Royce and Bentley

The author at the Rolls-Royce Foundation Museum in Mechanicsburg, Penn.
Photo by Sheila M. Lambert

Rolls-Royce Foundation
189 Hempt Road
Mechanicsburg, PA 17050
717-795-9400
www.rollsroycefoundation.org

The Rolls-Royce Foundation seeks donations of parts and parts cars to help maintain its museum collection of more than 20 Rolls-Royce and Bentley motorcars; extras are displayed and sold at an annual silent auction

Rolls-Royce Motor Cars NA, LLC
300 Chestnut Ridge Road
Woodcliff Lake, NJ 07677
877-877-3735
www.rolls-roycemotorcars.com

Provides parts for 2003 and later Rolls-Royce cars through its network of authorized dealers

Restorations and Specialist Repair Service

UNITED KINGDOM AND EUROPE

The **Rolls-Royce Bentley Specialists Association** is an organization founded in 1984 representing repair, service and restoration specialists primarily in the U.K., but also with international members in Europe, the United States and elsewhere. Member companies have to have worked at least five years predominantly on Rolls-Royce and Bentley motor cars and pass a stringent initial inspection. An annual review by the RRBSA is required. Visit their website at www.rrbsa.co.uk for a list of all members.

A&S Engineering
Unit 1, Wayside Park
Union Lane, Alton, Hants. GU34 2PJ, UK
44 (0)1420 541257

Alpine Eagle
The Mill
Little Clanfield, Oxfordshire OX18 2RX, U.K.
44 (0)1367 810401
www.aplineeagle.co.uk
Specialists in Derby and Crewe cars up to 1955

Classic Restorations (Scotland) Ltd.
Pitnacree Street
Alyth, Perthshire PH11 8DY, Scotland, U.K.
44 (0)1828 633293
www.classicrestorations.co.uk
Restorations, repair and servicing of Rolls-Royce and Bentley cars through 1998 model year

Fiennes Restoration
Broughton Poggs Business Park
Filkins, Oxon GL7 3JHX, U.K.
44 (0)1367 810438
www.fiennes.co.uk
Restoration of pre-1955 vehicles

Gary H. Wright Coach Trimming
126 Tanners Drive
Blakelands, Milton Keynes, Bucks MK14 5BP U.K.
44 (0)1908 617774
Manufactures interior trim, leatherwork and carpets for Rolls-Royce and Bentley cars

Harvey Wash Ltd.
Coggeshall Road
Kelvedon, Colchester, Essex CO5 9PF, U.K.
44 (0)1376 571174

HillierHill
Unit 18, Stilebrook Road
Yardley Road Industrial Estate
Olney, Bucks, MK46 5EA, U.K.
44 (0)1234 713871
www.hillierhill.com
Specializes in post-war Rolls-Royce and Bentley restorations

Jack Barclay Service Centre
65 Burr Road
Wandsworth, London SW18 45Q, U.K.
44 (0)207 738 8333
www.hrowen.co.uk
A Bentley dealer for almost 90 years, Jack Barclay now has an on-line store, claimed to be the world's largest, of Bentley and Crewe-built Rolls-Royce parts from pre-1955 to the present

Jonathan Wood
Clockhouse Workshop
Finchingfield Road
Little Sampford, Saffron Walden, Essex CB10 2QN, U.K.
44 (0)1799 586888
www.jonathan-wood.co.uk
Mechanical repairs and restoration of pre-war Rolls-Royce and Bentley cars

BUY A CLASSIC ROLLS-ROYCE OR BENTLEY

Overton Vehicle Overhauls
370 Rayleigh Road
Eastwood, Essex SS9 5PP, U.K.
44 (0)1702 526152
www.bentleyboys.com
Specialists in Bentleys

P & A Wood
Pound Field, The Endway
Great Easton, Dunmow, Essex CM6 2HD, U.K.
44 (0)1371 870848
www.pa-wood.co.uk
Coachwork, parts and restoration for all Rolls-Royce and Bentley cars

UNITED STATES

Automotive International
6150A Old Pineville Road
Charlotte, NC 28217
704-521-2886
www.automotive-international.com
This well-respected shop, open since 2001, provides mechanical repairs, bodywork, paint and complete restoration on Rolls-Royce, Bentley and other vehicles including Ferrari and Maserati

Bentley High Point
1730 North Main Street
High Point, NC 27262
336-884-1100
www.bentleyhighpoint.com
Bentley High Point is one of the oldest continuously operating Bentley dealerships in the U.S.; the chief mechanic, Mel Robertson, has been working on Rolls-Royce and Bentley cars for 40 years

Bentley Zionsville
360 South First Street
Zionsville, IN 46077

317-873-2360

www.albersrollsbentley.com

Long-established and well-respected Bentley dealer and parts retailer for Crewe-built Rolls-Royce and Bentley cars

Dennison-Jayne Motors
322 South Concord Road
West Chester, PA 19382
610-436-8668

www.dennisonjaynemotors.com

Specializes in Phantom II and III and small horsepower Rolls-Royce and Bentley cars, member of Rolls-Royce Bentley Specialists Association

Doug Seibert's Garage
1291 Clifford Avenue
Rochester, NY 14621
585-325-7393

Provides specialty machining and other repairs and restoration on Silver Clouds and other cars

Enfield Auto Restoration
4 Print Shop Road
Enfield, CT 06082
860-749-7917

www.enfieldautorestoration.com

Besides restoration, Enfield also offers some custom-made Rolls-Royce parts

The Frawley Company
138 Main Street
Parkesburg, PA 19365
610-857-1099

www.thefrawleycompany.com

Specializes in repair and restoration of Silver Ghost through Silver Shadow and Bentley T-Series cars

Hilborn Motor Car Interiors
1460 Gemini Boulevard, #4

Orlando, FL 32837
407-803-3778
www.hilbornmotorcar.com
Specializes in leather seat upholstery, carpet sets, headliners and lambs wool floor overlays for Rolls-Royce

J.E. Robison Service
347 Page Boulevard
Springfield, MA 01104
413-785-1665
www.robisonservice.com
Well-known service center for post-war Rolls-Roll, Bentley and other high-end automobiles

Palma Classic Cars
529 West Kings Highway
Audubon, NJ 08106
856-547-6522
www.palmaclassiccars.com
Well-known repair and restoration specialist, active in RROC; John Palma is a technical consultant for RROC on 1955 and later Rolls-Royce and Bentley cars

Pollock Auto Restoration
Pottstown, PA 19464
610-323-7108
www.pollockauto.com

NS Refinishing
3186 Irishtown Road
Gordonville, PA 17529
717-768-0751
www.nswoodrefinishing.com
Specializes in interior veneer repairs and refinishing

Sam Smyth Imported Car Service, Inc.
8773 Remington Road
Cincinnati, OH 45242

513-793-0434
www.smythimports.com

Vantage Motorworks, Inc.
1898 N.E. 151 Street
North Miami, FL 33162
305-940-1161
www.vantagemotorworks.com

Vintage & Auto Rebuild
121 Industrial Parkway
Chardon, OH 44024
440-285-2742
www.ghostparts.com
Specializes in Silver Ghost and other pre-1930 parts

The Vintage Garage
Consolidated Farms Barn
111 North Hollow Road
Stowe, VT 05672
802-253-9256
www.vintagegarage.com
Member of Rolls-Royce Bentley Specialists Association, active in RROC

White Post Restorations
One Old Car Drive
White Post, VA 22663
540-837-1140
www.whitepost.com
Specializes in brake work and does other repairs and restoration

Zenith Motor Co.
11433 East Truman Road
Independence, MO 64050
816-785-9656
www.zenithmoco.com
Offers Rolls-Royce and Bentley service and restoration

Technical Consultants

The Rolls-Royce Owners' Club (www.rroc.com) maintains a list of nearly 40 technical consultants, experts in various areas of Rolls-Royce and Bentley matters, from specialists in individual models such as early and late Silver Ghosts, Derby Bentley, Phantom I, II, III, Silver Clouds, Silver Shadows, Silver Spirits/Spurs to experts in leather, woodwork, coachwork, bearings, electrical systems, GM Hydramatic transmissions, tires and other components. There is no charge for consultation with these valuable experts, but to use their services you must be an RROC member.

Transport

Reliable Carriers, Inc.
41555 Koppernick Road
Canton, MI 48187
800-521-6393
www.reliablecarriers.com

Reliable Carriers is North America's largest enclosed auto transport company, serving the United States (lower 48 states only) and all provinces of Canada

Dictionary of Rolls-Royce and Bentley Terms

Here are definitions of commonly used terms in the world of Rolls-Royce and Bentley motorcars.

Accumulator Refers to a storage reservoir in which hydraulic fluid is held under pressure; the accumulator is part of the complex braking system of the Rolls-Royce Silver Shadow and Silver Spirit series and their derivatives.

Antique Although there is no universally agreed-upon definition, and different countries and U.S. states have different definitions of what legally constitutes antique vehicles, an antique automobile generally is considered one that is at least 25 to 35 years old. See also Brass-Era, Classic, Vintage and Veteran.

Badge An insignia, logo or mascot that represents the brand -- for example, the entwined double Rs of the Rolls-Royce logo, the Spirit of Ecstasy figure on the Rolls-Royce radiator or the Flying B symbol of the Bentley.

Barn Find Refers to a vehicle discovered in a barn or other storage building. Often a barn-find vehicle has been left undriven for years and may require considerable restoration and repair.

Blatchley, John Polwhele A designer and stylist for Rolls-Royce from 1940 to 1969, and chief styling engineer from 1955 to 1969, J. P. Blatchley was responsible for the look of some of the most iconic Rolls-Royce and Bentley cars of the last half of the 20th century, including the Rolls-Royce Silver Cloud and Bentley S-Series and the Rolls-Royce Silver Shadow and Bentley T-Series. He also is credited with the design of the original Rolls-Royce Corniche and was involved in the design of early post-World War II vehicles including the Bentley Mark V and Rolls-Royce Silver Dawn. Blatchley retired in 1969 and died in 2008.

Bentley Motors Limited The company by this name dates to 1919, when it was incorporated by its founder, W. O. Bentley. It continued as the Bentley division of Rolls-Royce when it was absorbed by Rolls-Royce Limited in 1931, after Bentley failed financially due to the impact of the Great Depression. It is the direct successor of Rolls-Royce Motors Limited, the company that was formed in the early 1970s when the Rolls-Royce motorcars and aircraft engine were separated by a receiver and shortly thereafter became divisions of Vickers. Volkswagen AG bought Bentley Motors Limited in 1998. It remains today as the name of VW's Bentley group.

Big Five The five largest and most important British coachbuilders: Park Ward, H. J. Mulliner, James Young, Hooper and Freestone & Webb.

Bonnet British term for the hood of a car.

Boot British term for the trunk of a car.

Brass-Era Car Usage differs but many car collectors used Brass-Era to refer to vehicles produced from around 1904 to 1919, which includes the Rolls-Royce 40/50 or Silver Ghost. The name comes from the prominent brass fittings that were used for radiators, lamps and other parts on vehicles of the time.

Classic Car Usually used for collectible vehicles of at least 20 to 25 years old. See also Antique, Brass-Era, Vintage and Veteran.

Coachbuilders Companies that specialized, as early as the 17th or early 18th century, in building the bodies of horse carriages, and then from the early 20th century in building the bodies of motorcars, especially luxury motorcars such as Rolls-Royce and Bentley. Until the 1940s, Rolls-Royce manufactured only the "rolling chassis," the chassis, engine and mechanical parts from the instrument panel forward, while coachbuilders such as James Young, Park Ward, Hooper, H. J. Mulliner and others produced the body and interior of the vehicles. In some cases, the coachbuilders were independent of Rolls-Royce, while in others the coachbuilders were, or later became, subsidiaries or divisions of Rolls-Royce. The introduction in 1965 by Rolls-Royce of unitary or monocoque construction on most of its lines marked the end of the most of the British coachbuilders, although some coachbuilt models of Rolls-Royce and Bentley were produced for a few decades afterward.

Coachbuilt Referring to a Rolls-Royce or Bentley motorcar with a body and interior built by a coachbuilder such as Hooper, H. J. Mulliner or James Young.

Concours d'Elegance From the French for Competition of Elegance, an automobile show to determine the most elegant or beautiful. Among the best known and most prestigious of these shows are Pebble Beach *Concours d'Elegance*, Amelia Island *Concours d'Elegance* and the Meadow Brook *Concours d'Elegance*. A Rolls-Royce or Bentley in *"Concours"* condition is considered one of the best cars of its type in the country or world, capable of winning a major show competition.

Connolly Refers to a type of top-grain leather from the Connolly Leather company, established in England in 1878. Connolly leather is used for seats and other interior finishings of Rolls-Royce and Bentley cars, along with

Jaguar, Aston Martin, Land Rover and others. It also was used for seats in the Concorde supersonic jets and for Mies Van Der Rohe's original Barcelona chairs. Connolly Leather tried to expand into the United States in the 1990s but failed, and the company went out of business. However, in 2003 a member of the Connolly family established a new company, CB Leather Ltd., and now provides Connolly leather for premium automobiles and other products.

Corniche A two-door coupe originally based on the Silver Shadow that was produced by Rolls-Royce beginning in 1971. Initially the Corniche came in a hardtop coupe and a convertible version, called the drophead, but in later years only the convertible version was produced. Corniche is from the French for a road along the side of a cliff, especially a coastal road and particularly the road from near Nice to Monaco.

Crewe A town and railroad junction in Cheshire East, England, Crewe was the site of the Rolls-Royce aviation engines during World War II and the main Rolls-Royce and Bentley motorcar production facility from 1945-46 until 2002. Some 70,000 Rolls-Royce cars were built here. In addition, around 31,000 Bentleys were manufactured here, not including those built after the purchase in 1998 by Volkswagen AG. Vehicles produced here, especially Rolls-Royces, are referred to by enthusiasts as "Crewe-built." The Bentley division of Volkswagen took over and expanded the Crewe facility in 1998, eventually more than doubling the workforce. Production of Bentleys continues here to the present day, although much of the engineering and design is now done in Germany.

Daily Driver Refers to a Rolls-Royce or Bentley that is used for regular transportation, rather than just as a collectible or show car.

Derby Pronounced "Darby," Derby is city in the East Midlands region of England. Because it was the site of Lombe's Mill, a silk throwing mill built in the early 18th century, the first fully mechanized factory in the world, Derby is often considered as the place of origin of the Industrial Revolution. Charles Royce and Henry Rolls opened a factory here in 1907 to manufacture Rolls-Royce motorcars and, later aircraft engines. Rolls-Royce (the famous Silver Ghost was manufactured here beginning in 1908) and Bentley vehicles (from 1933) were manufactured there until the opening of the new Crewe motor car factory in 1945-1946. A total of more than 19,000 Rolls-Royce and nearly 2,500 Bentleys were built at Derby. Large numbers of Rolls-Royce aircraft engines also were built at Derby during World War I and World War II, and jet engine manufacturing continues at Derby up to the present day, under Rolls-Royce Holdings PLC.

Division The panel that separates the front and rear seats of luxury cars such as Rolls-Royce and Bentley. In chauffeur-driven vehicles it serves to separate the driver in front from the passengers in the rear. In most cases, the division includes a glass section. Vehicles with a division are much sought-after by collectors.

Drophead Coupé The term drophead coupe or coupé refers to a two-door, four-seater convertible sportscar; a soft top convertible.

Estate Car Refers to a station wagon-type of body originally used as a "shooting car," a car to carry country gentlemen, their guns and their dogs to a hunt. A number of custom coachbuilders *(q.v.)* built estate car bodies that were fitted on Rolls-Royce or Bentley chassis.

Everflex A British fabric, polyvinyl chloride, similar to what is often just called vinyl, popular on luxury cars, especially Rolls-Royce, Bentley and Jaguar, from the 1960s to 1990s. It is used to cover the metal roof of the vehicle. On Rolls-Royces, it was best known for its use on Silver Shadow (along with Bentley T-type models) in the 1970s, but it also was used on Silver Spirit and Silver Spur and their derivatives from 1980 on. The most commonly used colors on Rolls-Royce were grey, light blue and brown, but many other colors were available as options. On some vehicles with Everflex roofs, moisture eventually gets between the fabric and the steel roof, causing a rust problem. Heat from the sun also can impact the Everflex covering, causing it to pull away from the car body.

Fascia A chiefly British term for dashboard or instrument panel.

Goodwood A town in West Sussex, England, that is the world headquarters and an assembly plant for Rolls-Royce motorcars produced by a division of BMW AG since 2003. Goodwood also is home to a famous automobile and motorcycle racing course, Goodwood Circuit, which dates from 1948.

Freestone & Webb Founded in 1923, this London-based coachbuilder was one of the "big five" coachbuilders to remain in business after World War II. The company was slow to accept changes, sticking with wood frames from South African ash and avoiding all-steel bodies right up to the sale and closing of the company in 1958. Most of their bodies were one-off designs.

H. J. Mulliner This prestigious coachbuilder dates back to 1760, when it was founded in Northhampton. Henry Jervis Mulliner purchased the business, which had relocated to London, in 1900. It soon established a relationship with Rolls-Royce. H. J. Mulliner was the founder of the Automobile Club of Great Britain and Ireland, later the Royal Automobile Club. The Mulliner company is especially known for its work in the 1930s, when it developed the "high vision" concept for Rolls-Royce bodies, involving a larger expanse of glass windows. Mulliner was also known for its interiors, which often featured a particular kind of walnut veneer, called flame walnut, with boxwood stringing and inlays of silver or pewter. In the post-World War II period, when wood for coach bodies was in short supply, Mulliner moved to a composite wood and metal body and then to all-metal with extensive use of light-weight aluminum alloys. In the 1950s, Mulliner was known for its beautiful Bentley Continental coachwork, now highly sought-after by collectors. The firm was acquired by Rolls-Royce in 1959, and in 1961 Mulliner was merged into another Rolls-Royce firm, Park Ward, becoming Mulliner Park Ward.

Hooper & Co. This well-known coachbuilder dates back to 1807 and the establishment of London firm J. & G. Adams. George Hooper became a partner in the firm in 1830, and after the death of George Adams in 1846 it became known as Hooper & Co. With the advent of automobiles in the early 20th century, Hooper turned its attention to building bodies for motorcars, mainly for Rolls-Royce and Daimler. Hooper held Royal Warrants to build coaches for British royalty for 130 years, through the reigns of seven kings and queens. The firm closed in 1959.

James Young Coachbuilder established in Bromley, England, in 1863. In 1908 the firm built its first automobile body, and from 1921 the company built motorcar bodies for Rolls-Royce and Bentley. In 1937, the company was purchased by the London Rolls-Royce dealer, Jack Barclay, which remains in business today. James Young produced its last bodies in 1968 or the Phantom V.

Mascot A figure or other symbol first used in the early 1900s by owners to give their motorcars a distinctive look (*q.v.* **Badge**). The Rolls-Royce "Spirit of Ecstasy," a figure of a woman leaning forward designed by sculptor Charles Robinson Sykes that was placed on the top of the radiator of Rolls-Royce motorcars was introduced by Rolls-Royce around 1911 so that owners would not disfigure their vehicles with various mascots of their own design. The less well-known "Flying B" of Bentley is another mascot.

Monocoque From the French word for single hull or single shell, monocoque (pronounced "mono-coke") refers to a construction style of automobiles where the body and chassis of the vehicle are integrated and unitary, rather than having a separate chassis with the body attached to it. This type of construction, common on most modern cars today, has been used by Rolls-Royce since 1965 with the introduction of the Silver Shadow series.

Mulliner Park Ward Two long-established coachbuilders Park Ward, which Rolls-Royce bought in 1939, and H. J. Mulliner, which was acquired by Rolls-Royce in 1959, were merged in 1961 as Mulliner Park Ward. They became the coachbuilding arm of Rolls-Royce and Bentley, first in London and after 1992 at Crewe.

Owner-Driver Refers to the (usually) smaller Rolls-Royce and Bentley models that were designed to be driven by the owner rather than by a chauffeur. These vehicles typically had no division. Examples of classic owner-driver Rolls-Royces include the Rolls-Royce Twenty, 20/25, 25/30, Silver Cloud, Silver Shadow and Silver Spirit/Silver Spur models, along with smaller post-2002 BMW/Rolls-Royce models such as Ghost and Wraith.

Park Ward Noted coachbuilder founded in North London in 1919 by William MacDonald Park and Charles Ward, Park Ward won early fame for its Bentley bodies. By the mid-1920s it was doing custom coach bodies for both Rolls-Royce and Bentley. When Rolls-Royce Limited took over Bentley in 1931, it acquired a stake in Park Ward. In 1939, Rolls-Royce bought the remaining interest in Park Ward. Park Ward created some of the most elegant and distinctive bodies ever produced for Rolls-Royce and Bentley cars. Also, Park Ward's experience in building all-steel bodies for Bentley vehicles was important in Rolls-Royce's move to a "rationalised" production system using steel bodies for the Bentley Mark VI, Rolls-Royce Silver Dawn and particularly the Silver Cloud. Park Ward and H. J. Mulliner, which had been acquired by Rolls-Royce in 1959, came together in London as Mulliner Park Ward in 1961. Thereafter, the combined company was the coachbuilding arm of Rolls-Royce and Bentley, first in London and after 1991/1992 at Crewe.

Phantom Phantom is the name given to several Rolls-Royce models, including the New Phantom introduced in 1925 (later called the Phantom I), Phantom II in 1929, Phantom III in 1936, Phantom IV in 1950, Phantom V in 1959 and Phantom VI in 1968. The Phantom IV was one of the most exclusive models ever built by Rolls-Royce, with only 18 cars delivered, all but one to royalty and heads of state. The Phantoms V and VI, though produced in greater numbers, were also large, luxurious, chauffeur-driven vehicles. In the 21st century, the Phantom was the first Rolls-Royce produced by the BMW-owned Rolls-Royce Motor Cars, with the first one manufactured in 2003. Currently, BMW/Rolls-Royce has four top-of-the-line Phantom models, including the Phantom, the Phantom Extended Wheelbase, which sells for around $550,000, the Phantom Coupé and the convertible Phantom Drophead Coupé.

Pressed Steel Co. Ltd. An automobile body pressing and assembly firm established in Cowley near Oxford in 1926 initially providing bodies for Morris Motors. It became independent of Morris in 1930, becoming Britain's largest independent automobile body supplier. In 1946 Rolls-Royce Limited selected Pressed Steel to make the all-steel bodies for the Bentley Mark VI and in 1949 for the Rolls-Royce Silver Dawn. Rolls-Royce also contracted with Pressed Steel to make the bodies for the Silver Cloud beginning in the mid-1950s and the monocoque bodies for the Silver Shadow beginning in the mid-1960s. In the 1950s Pressed Steel was the largest company of its type in Europe. In 1965 Pressed Steel was acquired by British Motor Corporation, maker of Morris and Austin vehicles, and was merged into BMC's Fisher and Ludlow subsidiary, becoming Pressed Steel Fisher.

Pre-War, Post-War As commonly used in the Rolls-Royce and Bentley context, pre-war refers to vehicles made before World War II, generally 1939 and earlier, and post-war refers to vehicles made from 1946 onward.

Rolling Chassis The chassis, engine and mechanical parts from the instrument panel forward of a Rolls-Royce or Bentley built by Rolls-Royce. The body and interior of the vehicle would be built by a coachbuilder *(q.v.)* and fitted to the rolling chassis by Rolls-Royce.

Rolls-Royce Limited The corporate name of the company formed by Charles Rolls and Henry Royce on March 15, 1906, to build Rolls-Royce motor cars. Later, the company also built aircraft engines and Bentley cars. In 1971, as a result of the high cost of developing a new jet aircraft engine, Rolls-Royce Limited was nationalized by the British government as Rolls-Royce (1971) Limited *(q.v)*. In 1973, Rolls-Royce (1971) Limited motorcars was separated from the aero division. The car company was then called Rolls-Royce Motors Limited, while the aircraft engine division continued as Rolls-Royce (1971) Limited until 1987 when it was re-privatized as Rolls-Royce PLC.

Rolls-Royce (1971) Limited The nationalized company formed in 1971 from Rolls-Royce Limited when the aircraft engine division became seriously troubled financially attempting to develop a new jet engine for Lockheed. In 1973, Rolls-Royce (1971) Limited motorcars was separated from the aero division and called Rolls-Royce Motors Limited.

Rolls-Royce Motors Limited The company formed in 1973 when Rolls-Royce (1971) Limited was separated from the aircraft engine division of Rolls-Royce. Limited is often abbreviated Ltd.

Rolls-Royce Motor Cars This is the modern company, officially established in 1998 by BMW AG to license the Rolls-Royce name and principal trademarks. However, actual production by BMW of its first Rolls-Royce vehicle, the Phantom, did not begin until 2003. Since then the company has additional other models, all based on BMW's German engineering and using BMW engines. The Rolls-Royce Motor Cars headquarters is in Goodwood, West Sussex, England. While Rolls-Royce vehicles are assembled at the Goodwood plant, design, engineering and much of the actual manufacturing are carried out at BMW facilities in Germany and elsewhere in continental Europe.

Rolls-Royce PLC The name given to Rolls-Royce aircraft engine manufacturing company when Rolls-Royce (1971) Limited was re-privatized in 1987.

Rolls, Charles Stewart Pioneer aviator and motorcar enthusiast, co-founder of Rolls-Royce Limited in 1906; born in London in 1877; was graduated from Cambridge; met Henry Royce in 1904; died 1910 in a flying accident.

Royce, Frederick Henry Sir Engineer, pioneering automobile builder, co-founder of Rolls-Royce Limited in 1906; born in Alwalton, Huntingdonshhire, England, in 1863; met Charles Rolls in 1904; received the OBE in 1918; was made a baronet, of Seaton, in 1930; died in 1933.

Silver Cloud Refers to a Rolls-Royce model introduced in April 1955 and produced at the Crewe facility, with various improvements, through March 1966. It had a steel-body produced by Pressed Steel Co. Ltd. (with higher quality steel than used in earlier post World War II models) and aluminum doors, bonnet and boot top. Silver Clouds with both Rolls-Royce and coachbuilt bodies were delivered. Using a 155-horsepower in-line six-cylinder engine, the Silver Cloud I had drum brakes, with twin master cylinders from 1956. Power steering and air-conditioning were optional from 1956. A Silver Cloud II with a mostly aluminum V-8 engine was introduced in 1958, and the Silver Cloud III, with an improved V-8 with hardened crankshaft and somewhat more power arrived in 1963. A total of 7,372 Silver Clouds were produced, including short and long wheelbase models and coachbuilt versions. The Bentley S-Series (S1, S2 and S3) produced during the same period in about the same numbers is very similar, essentially the same vehicle except with a different badge and different radiator grill.

Silver Ghost Refers to a famous early model of Rolls-Royce, initially called by the company the 40/50. It was built briefly at Rolls-Royce facilities in Manchester, and from 1908 at the Rolls-Royce plant in Derby *(q.v.)* and at the Rolls-Royce United States plant in Springfield, Mass. *(q.v.)*. A total of 7,876 Silver Ghosts were produced, including 1,703 in Massachusetts. The Silver Ghost name, used by the press and the public, was not officially recognized by the company until 1925. The name Silver Ghost also refers to one specific car ordered in 1907 by Managing Director Claude Johnson that the company called by that name (chassis number 60551, registered AX 201).

Silver Shadow Refers to a Rolls-Royce series and its derivatives that was produced from 1965 to 1980, the most popular line in Rolls-Royce history, with nearly 40,000 vehicles manufactured. The introduction of the Silver Shadow model marked the most extensive redesign and reengineering of the Rolls-Royce motorcar in the company's history to that date. Instead of a chassis and model style, it had a unibody or monocoque *(q.v.)* construction, integrating the chassis and the body. Another innovative feature was a high-pressure hydraulic braking system licensed from Citroën, using disc rather than drum brakes. It also had a hydraulic self-leveling suspension. The Silver Shadow was powered from 1965 to 1970 by a 6.2-liter V-8 producing 172 horsepower, and from 1970 to 1980 by a 6.7-liter V-8 putting out 189 horsepower. Most cars in the line had General Motors Hydrostatic transmissions. The body had a classic yet modern look, and while the Shadow was narrower and shorter than the Silver Cloud it replaced, it actually had more interior room. The original Shadow was sold primarily as an owner-driven automobile, although a long-wheelbase model, some with a division, was also offered. In 1975, the long-wheelbase version of the Shadow was renamed Silver Wraith II. The Silver Shadow II was introduced in 1977, with a new rack-and-pinion steering system and other evolutionary improvements. During the course of Shadow production, the Corniche model was introduced, with coupé and convertible versions. Also debuting (in 1975) was the Camargue, arguably the most-expensive production Rolls-Royce ever sold, selling for $147,000 when introduced, or nearly $640,000 in today's dollars. The Bentley version of the

Silver Shadow was the Bentley T-Series (T1 and T2), very similar to the Rolls-Royce in every way except the badge and the grill design. A total of 2,436 Bentley Ts were delivered, less than 10% of the production of the Rolls-Royce version.

Silver Spirit Refers to a series of vehicles launched by Rolls-Royce in 1980. Its derivatives, somewhat confusedly named and marketed, including the Silver Spur (a long wheelbase version of the Silver Spirit), Silver Spirit II and III, Silver Spur II and III, Flying Spur, Silver Dawn, New Silver Spirit and New Silver Spur, Silver Spur Touring Limousine and also the Bentley Mulsanne and Eight. The Silver Spirit line marked a further evolution of the Silver Shadow series, rather than a radical change. It continued to use the 6.7-liter V-8. One of the biggest changes was in a greatly improved ride control and self-leveling system, and the use of mineral oil rather than regular brake fluid in the braking and leveling system. Further performance and safety improvements were added as the years passed, such as a driver-side airbag and then passenger-side airbag. The last Silver Spirit was delivered in 1997 and the last Silver Spur in 2000. It was during the Silver Spirit period when Bentley, still owned by Rolls-Royce and produced at Crewe along with the Rolls-Royce models, regained its footings as an independent brand. The Bentley R Turbo, which debuted in 1985, was the notable model during this time, with 7,230 produced through 1997.

Silver Spur Refers to the long-wheelbase version of the Silver Spirit series. The original Silver Spur was introduced in 1980, the Silver Spur II in late 1989, the Silver Spur III in 1993 and the New Silver Spur in 1995. The last New Silver Spur was produced in 2000. There also was a limited-production Silver Spur Touring Limousine built from 1982 to 1999.

Silver Wraith Refers to the first post-World War II Rolls-Royce produced at the Crewe facility, with an output of 1,883 cars from 1946 to 1959. This was the last Rolls-Royce to be produced as a rolling chassis *(q.v.)* only, except for the large Phantom models. The Silver Wraith II was the long wheelbase version of the Silver Shadow manufactured starting in 1975 and otherwise not directly related to the original Silver Wraith.

Small Horsepower Usually refers to certain pre-World War II Rolls-Royce and Bentley motorcars, including the Rolls-Royce 20 hp, 20/25 hp, 25/30 hp and Bentley 3 ½-Liter and 4 ¼-Liter models.

Spirit of Ecstasy The figure of a woman leaning forward with her clothes billowing backward that has appeared on the radiator of Rolls-Royces for more than a century. Designed by sculptor Charles Robinson Sykes in 1910-1911, the figure is thought to be at least partly modeled on Eleanor Thornton, private secretary to and lover of the second Baron Montagu of Beaulieu. It is also known as the Flying Lady. It has appeared in at least 11 different versions on Rolls-Royce cars, including in a version where the figure is kneeling. The Spirit of Ecstasy is a trademark of Rolls-Royce.

Springfield This was the site of a Rolls-Royce manufacturing plant in the town of Springfield, Mass., that produced near 3,000 Silver Ghost and Phantom cars from 1920 until 1931. This is the only site outside of Great Britain where Rolls-Royce motorcars were manufactured. The remains of the factory were razed in 2011.

Veteran Car Usage varies but usually refers to vehicles from the late 19th and early 20th centuries, typically up to about 1919 or 1920. For Rolls-Royce, this mostly means earlier 40/50 hp vehicles, popularly called Silver Ghost, although some car enthusiasts limit Veteran to mean vehicles produced before around 1905, which would include early vehicles produced by Henry Royce. See also Antique, Brass-Era, Classic and Vintage.

Vickers Vickers PLC, a British engineering and armaments company with roots dating to 1828, acquired Rolls-Royce Motors Limited in 1980 and continued to own it until Vickers sold it to Volkswagen AG in 1998.

VIN Vehicle Identification Number, an international system of identifying a specific automobile or truck using a unique 17-place identifier code. It was first used in 1954, but there was no universal system until 1980, when it was required by the United States National Highway Traffic Safety Administration to be used by all vehicle manufacturers. Rolls-Royce and Bentley began using it that year, when the Silver Spirit series was introduced, although the company continued to use its own chassis number system as well.

Vintage Car Usage varies but usually refers to collectible cars from the pre-World War II period, especially from around 1919 to 1939. See also Antique, Brass-Era, Classic and Veteran.

Wings British term for fenders.

Bibliography

Scores, perhaps hundreds, of books have been written about Rolls-Royce and Bentley. Here are a few of them. Note that many books on these motorcars were published in small editions and are now out-of-print, available only from used book sellers, with the more rare volumes sometimes at high prices of several hundred dollars.

Abbiss, Reg, *The Bentley Story*, The History Press, Gloucestershire, U.K., 2014, 128 pp. Part of The Story series from The History Press, this little volume (just 5 by 7 inches in size) has color photographs in small format but is otherwise of limited interest to enthusiasts.

-- *The Rolls-Royce Story*, The History Press, Gloucestershire, U.K., 2012, 128 pp. Mostly focuses on Rolls-Royce history up to about 1960.

Bennett, Martin, *Rolls-Royce & Bentley The Crewe Years*, Haynes Publishing, Somerset, U.K. 3rd ed., 2011, 488 pp. This lavishly illustrated and meticulously researched work on motorcars built at Crewe from 1945 to 2002 is the best book covering this period. It is a heavy, coffee table-size volume, with a retail price of $110, with hundreds of superb photos in color and black-and-white.

-- *Rolls-Royce, The History of the Car*, Arco Publishing Co., New York, first published 1974, reprinted 1976 and 1978, 179 pp. Another well-researched and well illustrated book by Martin Bennett, although it covers mostly the earlier models, with coverage ending during the Silver Shadow period.

Bobbitt, Malcolm, *Rolls-Royce Silver Shadow T-Series, The Essential Buyer's Guide*, Veloce Publishing, 2008, ebook edition 2013, 64 pp. This book is unusual in that it is basically a guide for anyone considering buying a Silver Shadow or Bentley T-Series vehicle. It goes into considerable detail on inspecting a car before purchase and on potential repair and restoration costs. However, it is not a price guide to the Shadow.

Cockerman, Paul W., *Rolls-Royce & Bentley, Classic Elegance*, Todtri Productions Limited, New York, 1999, 80 pp. Some beautiful photographs but limited coverage of modern cars.

Dalton, Lawrence, *Those Elegant Rolls-Royce*, Dalton Watson Ltd., London, 1967, reprinted 1970, 320 pp. Part of a series on classic automobiles, this first of two volumes on Rolls-Royce covers cars from 1907 to 1939, using about 700 black-and-white photos of bodies by the leading coachbuilders.

-- *Rolls-Royce, The Elegance Continues,* Dalton Watson Ltd., London, first pub. 1971, revised and reprinted 1977, 280 pp. This volume continues the theme of *Those Elegant Rolls-Royce,* with coverage of cars built from immediately following World War II to the Silver Shadow period. Using mostly black-and-white photographs and line drawings, the focus of this work is on the remaining coach-built cars.

Eves, Edward, *Rolls-Royce, 75 Years of Motoring Excellence,* Chartwell Books, Secaucus, NJ, 1979, 208 pp. Nicely illustrated with photographs, Eves uses the narrative form to tell the story of the first 75 years of Rolls-Royce, providing only limited technical data and production numbers that take up space in many books on Rolls-Royce.

Helig, John with Abbiss, Reg, *Rolls-Royce The Best Car in the World,* Chartwell Books, Edison, NJ, 1999, 128 pp. This coffee table book, with many stunning color photographs, provides a brief overview of Rolls-Royce and, despite the title, of Bentley up to the time when Volkswagen took over.

Kinney, Dave (publisher), *Hagerty Price Guide Collectible Cars 1946 Forward,* Hagerty's Cars That Matter LLC, Great Falls, VA, 2015 (revised and published three times a year), 603 pp. Arguably the best and most-comprehensive valuation guide to collectible cars from World War II onward, including Bentley and Rolls-Royce. Hagerty, which also sells auto insurance, provides year-by-year and model-by-model valuation estimates in four categories of condition, Fair, Good, Excellent and *Concours.* A one-year subscription (three price guides) is $40.

Robson, Graham, *Rolls-Royce and Bentley, Volume 1, Standard Production Models 1945-1965, A Collector's Guide,* Motor Racing Publications, Croydon, U.K., 1985, 144 pp. This is part of the Collector's Guide series on classic cars from Aston Martins to VWs. There are four volumes on Rolls-Royce and Bentley, all by Graham Robson, a former racing driver for Triumph and prolific automotive writer, authoring more than 100 books on various cars. This series is out of print, and some volumes are difficult to find. Volume 4 on the Silver Spirit and its derivatives is probably the most useful.

-- *Rolls-Royce and Bentley, Volume 2, Coachbuilt Models 1945-1985, A Collector's Guide,* Motor Racing Publications, Croydon, U.K., 1984, 144 pp.

-- *Rolls-Royce and Bentley,, Volume 3, Shadow, Corniche, Camargue 1965-1985, A Collector's Guide,* Motor Racing Publications, Croydon, U.K., 1984, 144 pp.

BUY A CLASSIC ROLLS-ROYCE OR BENTLEY

-- *Rolls-Royce and Bentley, Volume 4: Silver Spirit to Azure (1980-1998), A Collector's Guide,* Motor Racing Publications, Croydon, U.K., 1999, 128 pp.

-- *Rolls-Royce Silver Cloud, The Complete Story,* The Crowood Press Ltd., Rambury, Marlborough, Wiltshire, U.K., 2000, 192 pp. Excellent guide to the famous Silver Cloud and Bentley S-Series by the highly knowledgeable and prolific Graham Robson.

Tubbs, D. B., *The Rolls-Royce Phantoms,* Hamish Hamilton Ltd., London, 1964, 64 pp. This charming little book, listed as a monograph, is written with wit and grace. It covers the first five Phantoms: the New Phantom, Phantom II, III, IV and V.

About the Author

A former newspaper editor and marketing consultant in New Orleans, Lan Sluder is the author of more than a dozen books on travel, retirement and other subjects. Among his specialties are the country of Belize and the Western North Carolina mountains. His other recent books include *Fodor's Belize, Amazing Asheville, Play Bridge Today, Asheville Relocation, Retirement and Visitor Guide* and *Easy Belize*. He also has written books for Frommer's and Avalon/Moon and has contributed articles to many magazines and newspapers and other media around the world, including the TravelChannel.com, *Chicago Tribune, Where to Retire, Globe & Mail, New York Times, Miami Herald* and *Caribbean Travel & Life*.

Lan Sluder and spouse, Sheila M. Lambert, own a Crewe-built Rolls-Royce 1991 Silver Spur II long-wheelbase saloon. The original owner, according to Rolls-Royce Foundation documentation of warranty records, was Antonio Deinde Fernandez, a Nigerian-born, Cambridge-educated billionaire who from 1985 to 1999 was an ambassador to the United Nations from several African countries including Mozambique, Angola, Togo and the Central African Republic. This car is unusual in that according to a previous owner and his long-time Rolls-Royce mechanic it is has armoured doors, adding approximately 1,000 pounds to the standard weight of 5,080 pounds. It came with two car phones, one in the rear for the ambassador or family members and one in front for driver or bodyguard (both phones are still in place but are not used). The Spur's exterior is Dark Oyster, and the interior is Mushroom Connelly leather with burr walnut and boxwood inlay veneer and granite carpets with lamb's wool overlays. It has power adjustable seats in both front and rear and fold-out walnut picnic tables. Currently the car is 61,500 miles from new.

Sluder lives on a small mountain farm near Asheville, N.C., with his wife, an attorney. They have two adult children: Brooks Lambert-Sluder, assistant director of Peer Advising Programs at Harvard, and Rose Lambert-Sluder, a graduate teaching fellow and graduate student in the MFA fiction program at the University of Oregon.

Index

20/25, *13, 14, 17, 39, 51, 64, 96, 141, 145*
25/30, *13, 15, 39, 49, 64, 141, 145*
40/50, *See* Silver Ghost

A

ABS *See* brakes, ABS
accumulator, *136*
airbag, *30, 57, 76, 78, 145*
air-conditioning, *20, 26, 30, 49, 53, 61, 69, 72, 75, 78, 80, 81, 143*
antique (car), *87, 136*
appreciation, *56, 70, 73, 75, 79, 80, 82*
Asheville, *76, 97, 98, 150*
auctions, auto *90*
author, *2, 5, 49, 85, 91, 128, 150*
AutoTrader.com, *60, 62*

B

badges, *19, 43, 58*
Barker, *13, 15*
Bentayga SUV (Bentley), *36, 42*
Bentley Drivers Club, *93, 100, 125*
Bentley Mark V, *16, 39, 136*
Bentley Mark VI, *7, 11, 16, 18, 39, 49, 52, 67, 96, 141, 142*
Bentley Motors Ltd., *11, 15, 33, 35, 39, 51, 136*
Bentley, Warren Owen, *11*
Bibliography, *147-149*
Blatchley, John Polwhele, *79, 136*
BMW, *33, 34, 35, 36, 37, 41, 42, 44, 45, 52, 53, 57, 60, 67, 77, 102, 125, 139, 141, 142, 143*
bodies, steel, *11, 16, 17, 20, 55, 139, 141, 142*
Bond, James, *15, 49*
bonnet, *137*
boot, *137*
brakes, ABS, *29, 54, 75, 78*
brakes, disc, *23, 24, 25, 69, 72, 75, 78*
brakes, drum, *80, 81, 82, 143, 144*
Brass-Era (car), *136, 137, 146*

C

Camargue, *26, 29, 40, 41, 69, 71, 85, 144, 149*
CarFax, *57, 60, 93*
chassis numbers, *5, 84-86*
chassis, rolling, *10, 11, 13, 39, 84, 137, 142, 145*
classic (car), *6, 23, 34, 46, 48, 49, 53, 56, 57, 60, 61, 62, 63, 69, 74, 87, 88, 89, 90, 91, 101, 141, 144, 147, 148*
Classic Car Club of America, *101*
ClassicCars.com, *60, 62, 91, 92*
coachbuilders, *6, 11, 15, 16, 17, 18, 24, 55, 79, 137, 139, 141, 148*
Concours, *56, 63, 65, 66, 67, 68, 69, 70, 73, 80, 91, 99, 100, 137, 148*
Connolly leather, *20, 25, 34, 75, 78, 81, 137*
consultants, technical *59, 135*
Continental R, *32, 86*
Corniche, *23, 26, 28, 40, 41, 52, 55, 65, 69, 71, 82, 85, 136, 138, 144, 149*
coupés, *26, 51, 55, 82*
Crewe (factory), *15, 17, 20, 31, 32, 33, 34, 35, 36, 37, 39, 41, 42, 57, 69, 77, 78, 80, 83, 86, 125, 126, 127, 129, 130, 132, 138, 141, 143, 145, 147*

D

dealership, *8, 53, 59, 60, 61, 72, 91*
dealerships, authorized Bentley, *111-124*
dealerships, authorized Rolls-Royce, *102-110*
Derby (factory), *8, 10, 12, 13, 15, 39, 51, 129, 135, 138, 144*
Dictionary of Rolls-Royce and Bentley terms, *136-145*
division (between front and rear seats), *27, 28, 33, 41, 55, 62, 85, 136, 138, 139, 141, 142, 143, 144*
drophead, *22, 26, 51, 55, 69, 82, 138, 139*

E

eBay.com (*also* eBay, eBay Motoros), *57, 60, 62, 91, 92*
Edmunds, *8, 63*
Eight (Bentley), *32, 85*
engine number, *84*
enthusiasts' club, *6, 48, 58, 60, 84, 85, 87, 92, 94, 95, 125*
estate car, *139*
Everflex roof, *75, 79, 139*

F

Factors to Consider Before Buying, *51-54*
fascia, *25, 26, 37, 76, 78, 139*
Fernandez, Antonio Deinde (ambassador to the United Nations), *151*
financing, *87, 92*
fluid, hydraulic, *28, 41, 136*
Flying B, *136*
Flying Lady, *43, 44, 95, 98, 99, 146*
Flying Spur, *30, 36, 41, 76, 83, 145*
Founding of Rolls-Royce, *8*
Freestone & Webb, *137, 139*

G

General Motors, *18, 19, 25, 39, 71, 80, 144*
GM, *72, 73, 74, 75, 76, 77, 78, 81, 135*
Goodwood (factory), *35, 36, 37, 42, 139, 143*
Green Label (Bentley), *34*

H

H. J. Mulliner, *11, 13, 17, 18, 24, 40, 49, 55, 98, 137, 139, 141*
Hagerty Price Guide, *59, 63, 148*
Hemmings, *62, 91*
Hemmings.com, *60, 92*
History of Rolls-Royce and Bentley, *8-37*
Hooper, *11, 13, 14, 17, 18, 55, 66, 137, 140*
How Much Will You Pay?, *62-68*

I

injection, fuel, *29, 54, 74, 77, 83, 86*
inspection, *61, 63, 90, 92, 129*
insurance, *57, 61, 63, 87, 88, 89, 90, 92, 100, 148*

J

James Young, *11, 17, 22, 55, 137, 140*
Johnson, Claude Goodman, *10*

K

Kelley Blue Book, *62, 63*

L

Lambert, Sheila M., *2, 5, 7, 9, 14, 16, 20, 22, 24, 26, 40, 45, 66, 70, 76, 79, 96, 98, 128, 150*
left-hand drive, *18, 39, 54, 84, 86*
Lennon, John, *22, 49*
limousine, *22, 27, 39, 40, 51, 55, 69*
long-wheelbase, *20, 24, 27, 28, 30, 70, 71, 81, 144, 145, 150*
Luxury Junkyard, *94, 127*

M

maintenance, *48, 51, 53, 58, 59, 72, 73, 94*
Manchester, *8, 38, 51, 104, 114, 144*
mascot, *43, 136, 140*
mechanic, factory-certified, *53*
Median Asking Price, *64, 65, 67, 68*
Merlin aircraft engine, *27*
"Miss Agnes" (converted Rolls-Royce pickup owned by Travis McGee), *49*
monocoque, *23, 24, 40, 69, 137, 141, 142, 144*
Mulliner Park Ward, *140, 141*
Mulsanne, *28, 31, 32, 36, 41, 83, 86, 145*

N

NADA, *62, 63*
New Phantom *See* Phantom I
New Silver Spur, *52, 145*

O

Ogilvy, David, *22*
oil, mineral (for brakes), *28, 29, 41, 73, 75, 78, 145*
Orlando, *97, 98*
Owners of Rolls-Royce and Bentley cars, *46-50*

P

Park Ward, *11, 13, 17, 22, 24, 27, 55, 137, 140, 141*
parts, sources of, *125-128*
Performance, *71, 74, 78, 81*
Phantom (Phantoms I-VI and also BMW-era Phantoms), *12, 13, 14, 15, 18, 19, 22, 27, 35, 36, 37, 39, 40, 42, 44, 49, 50, 51, 64, 66, 67, 69, 85, 86, 96, 132, 135, 140, 141, 143, 145, 146, 149*
Phantom I (New Phantom), *12, 13*
Phantom II, *12, 13, 39, 50, 132, 141, 149*
Phantom III, *13, 14, 15, 39, 49, 141*
Phantom IV, *18, 19, 39, 51, 69, 141*
Phantom V, *22, 36, 40, 49, 66, 85, 140, 141*
Phantom VI, *27, 66, 85, 86, 141*
picnic tables, *20*
power-assisted steering *See* steering, power
Preface, *5*
Pressed Steel Company, *16, 20, 80, 142, 143*
Pricing Rules of Thumb, *55-57*

Q

Queen Elizabeth II, *18, 22*

R

receivership, *28, 41*
Red Label (Bentley), *34*
repairs, *6, 10, 51, 53, 59, 63, 70, 72, 77, 131, 132, 134*
restoration, *6, 48, 51, 52, 53, 58, 59, 63, 72, 94, 127, 129, 131, 132, 133, 134, 135, 136, 147*
right-hand drive, *25, 85, 86*

Rolls, Charles, *10, 38, 39, 142, 143*
Rolls-Royce (1971) Limited, *142, 143*
Rolls-Royce and Bentley dealerships, *102-124*
Rolls-Royce Bentley Specialists Association, *132, 134*
Rolls-Royce Enthusiasts' Club, *58, 62, 89, 93, 99, 125*
Rolls-Royce Foundation, *96, 99, 128, 151*
Rolls-Royce Limited (or, Rolls-Royce Ltd.), *8, 15, 17, 23, 27, 28, 31, 33, 37, 38, 41, 136, 141, 142, 143*
Rolls-Royce Motor Cars, *102, 103, 104, 105, 106, 107, 108, 109, 110, 111, 128, 142, 143*
Rolls-Royce Motors Ltd., *28, 30, 32, 33, 37, 41, 42, 136, 142,143, 146*
Rolls-Royce Owners' Club, *58, 62, 88, 93, 95, 96, 98, 101, 125, 135*
Rolls-Royce PLC, *28, 142, 143*
Royce, Henry, *8, 10, 27, 38, 142, 143, 146, 148*
R-Type (Bentley), *52*

S

Selling Your Car, *94*
Shah of Iran, *22*
Silver Cloud I, II and III, *19, 20, 21, 23, 36, 39, 48, 49, 52, 56, 58, 65, 69, 79, 80, 81, 82, 84, 98, 136, 141, 142, 143, 144, 149*
Silver Dawn, *11, 16, 18, 31, 39, 42, 65, 136, 141, 142, 145*
Silver Ghost, *8, 9, 10, 11, 12, 38, 51, 64, 69, 84, 133, 134, 137, 138, 144, 146 See also* 40/50
Silver Seraph, *33, 34, 42, 57, 67*
Silver Shadow I and II, *23, 24, 25, 27, 28, 40, 41, 48, 49, 52, 56, 58, 65, 69, 70, 71, 72, 73, 75, 80, 82, 133, 136, 138, 139, 141, 142, 144, 145, 147, 148*
Silver Spirit and Silver Spirit II and III, *28, 29, 30, 31, 32, 41, 42, 48, 52, 54, 56, 66, 67, 73, 74, 75, 76, 77, 78, 80, 82, 85, 136, 139, 141, 145, 146, 148, 149*
Silver Spur, Silver Spur II and III, *5, 30, 31, 41, 52, 75, 76, 77, 78, 85, 86, 145, 150*
Silver Wraith and Silver Wraith II, *17, 18, 71, 145*
Sluder, Lan, *1, 2, 150*
Sources of Parts, Restoration, Repairs and Other Information, *125-135*
specialists (in Rolls-Royce and Bentley repairs), *59, 61,* 129-134
Spirit of Ecstasy, *43, 44, 45, 136, 140, 145 See also* Flying Lady
Springfield (factory), *10, 12, 13, 39, 59, 96, 133, 144, 146*
S-Series (Bentley), *48, 58, 68, 80, 136, 144, 149*
steering, power, *19, 49, 53, 69, 78, 81*
steering, rack-and-pinion, *25, 71, 72, 78, 144*
S-Type (Bentley), *19, 20, 21, 39*
Suggested Models for First-Time Buyers, *69-83*
suspension, *17, 23, 24, 28, 32, 41, 49, 61, 72, 75, 78, 83, 144*
Sykes, Charles Robinson, *43,140*
SZ series, *31, 73, See also* Silver Spirit and Silver Spur

T

Table of Contents, *3-4*

technical consultants, *59, 135*
The Yellow Rolls-Royce, 50
Thrupp & Baberly, *13*
Time Line (Rolls-Royce and Bentley History), *38-42*
Touring Limousine (Rolls-Royce), *30, 77, 86, 145*
transmission, automatic, *18, 25, 69, 73, 78, 80*
transport, *135*
T-Type (Bentley), *23, 24, 25, 40, 58, 69, 71, 133, 136, 145, 147*
Turbo R (Bentley), *32, 41, 49, 52, 68, 83, 85*
turbocharged, *30, 32, 36, 41, 76, 83, 86*
Twelve Steps to Buying a Rolls-Royce or Bentley, *58-61*
Twenty (Rolls-Royce), *13, 39, 51, 141*

V

V-12 engine, *13, 33, 34, 35*
V-8 engine, *18, 19, 22, 23, 30, 34, 36, 40, 41, 42, 49, 54, 69, 71, 72, 73, 74, 75, 77, 78, 79, 80, 81, 82, 83, 143, 144, 145*
Valuation Considering Condition, *63, 64, 65, 66, 67, 68*
Vehicle Identification Number (VIN), *41, 57, 84, 85, 146*
veneer, walnut, *34, 140*
veteran (car), *6, 53, 87*
Vickers, *28, 32, 33, 41, 42, 136, 146*
vintage (car), *6, 48, 49, 51, 53, 87, 95, 99*
VintageDrivingMachines.com, *60, 62*
Volkswagen, *15, 26, 32, 33, 34, 35, 36, 37, 42, 45, 57, 70, 77, 83, 136, 138, 146, 148*

W

Wilson carpets, *25, 34, 75, 78*
windows, power, *75, 78, 80, 81*
Winged B, *44*
wings, *146*
Wraith, *15, 17, 18, 20, 27, 28, 36, 37, 39, 40, 41, 49, 69, 71, 141, 144, 145*

www.ingramcontent.com/pod-product-compliance
Lightning Source LLC
Chambersburg PA
CBHW071723090426
42738CB00009B/1857